990
FRI
DUE   T- 21516

Frisbie, Florence
The Frisbies of the South Seas.

Date Due			

● Nukahiva

Tahuata

Futa Hiwa

UESAS

sappointment

Akahaina

Raiatea

IETY

a-Puka ●

nego

TU

Hull

● Rimit

TUE

THE FRISBIES OF THE SOUTH SEAS

Florence

(Johnny) Frisbie

THE FRISBIES
OF THE SOUTH SEAS

ILLUSTRATED BY TOM DUNN

1959

DOUBLEDAY & COMPANY, INC.

GARDEN CITY, NEW YORK

Prologue

An ocean wave is born thousands of miles away. Spawned in the cold waters of the north, it is pushed and molded by squall winds and accumulates energy for its long travel south. As the wave reaches maturity, its long swell changes from slate gray to frothy green and finally to tropic blue as it races to meet its appointment with a coral reef on an insignificant speck of atoll in the South Pacific. The reef welcomes yet resists the crushing power that moves over it with an exploding roar that mingles with the moaning sighs of the palm trees lining the shore.

The sound is barely noticed by the natives going about. But it is a large wave and the crash causes one or two to glance seaward, to watch the towering curtain of spray that hangs over the reef. Through the mist can be seen a sail several miles out and coming downwind.

Aboard the schooner *Tagua* a man is gazing with hungry eyes at the approaching land. He, too, is keeping an appointment with a speck of atoll which he has never before seen but which has come to be his biggest goal in life.

He has just finished writing to his mother, telling her: "I want a home, mother, on one of these beautiful little islands where I can sit back with my literary work and forget the need of further scheming for existence. . . . I wrote you before telling you that I was sailing for Puka-Puka [Danger Island]. We are nearing that land now, and [soon] I will be landed with a few cases of trade goods and left isolated on the loneliest island in the world."

Introduction

Robert Dean Frisbie was born in 1896, in Cleveland, Ohio, the son of Arthur Grazly Frisbie, a Quaker who later became a Four Square Gospelist, a Theosophist, a Christian Scientist, and a member of the Order of the Magi. Arthur was related to the great Ford family on his maternal side. Robert's mother, Florence Benson, was an unselfish woman from Vermont. When Robert was twelve he and his older brother, Charles, were placed in a somewhat monastic and Spartan school at Point Loma, California, called Raja Yoga Academy. There, for four years, they boarded while their father transacted his real estate business around the country and lectured on theosophy. The boys slept on pillowless beds, arose at six o'clock seven days a week, and followed this by vigorous military drill before breakfast, which, like all their other meals, was eaten in silence. They were not allowed to read a paper or see anything of the outside world except for two hours a week when they visited their parents. At no time were they taught religion. But somewhere along the way Robert revolted against religious authority, perhaps because of the fact that his father's lectures were generally negative and directed against the religions in which he previously, so praisingly, had believed. (For a while his father actually managed the affairs of Aimee Semple McPherson.) These deviations impressed young Robert so much that many years later he still felt joy in exposing the phoniness and hypocrisy of many religious leaders.

But even as a young boy Robert was naturally quiet and shy and tended to be non-social. He read a great deal from the books in the family library and often wrote long poems in friendly competition with his brother. Many of these poems were dedicated to his mother, whom he loved very deeply. She seemed to understand the thoughts and ambitions of her son much better than did her strict and unbending husband. This close relationship lasted till her death in 1942, carried on largely by a voluminous correspondence. Robert's letters to his mother reveal the deep obligation he felt for her encouragement and support of his work, which was painfully slow in being accepted by the public. Of her letters to him there is no record, as they were destroyed in the great hurricane on Suwarrow the year of her death.

While stationed with the United States 8th Cavalry in Texas during the World War I, he wrote a lengthy free verse poem to his mother, from which this excerpt, as well as many of his letters, expresses his strong feeling for her:

Never will another be
So faithful a companion—
Mother mine.

Robert was a frail child, tall and thin, like his mother. He was particularly susceptible to respiratory illness, and was in fact medically discharged from the Army with tuberculosis in 1918. The resulting forty-five-dollar-a-month pension was to be, in later years, the difference between starvation and a comfortable existence in the South Pacific.

However, in spite of his physical limitations Robert developed a keen desire for adventure. He left home when he was sixteen to "strike out for myself." He read every bit of literature he could find concerning the South Seas. Robert Louis Stevenson was his idol. It is little wonder that when the examining army doctor told Pvt. Frisbie his lungs needed a complete change of climate the young man's thoughts turned to the picture of the sunlit beauty of the South Seas he carried in his mind.

His desire to leave America became an obsession, and he bent every effort in that direction. He cared little about his friends and lost all interest in advancing his education. He had a certain contempt for formal schooling anyway, feeling that American high schools had failed to keep him interested in learning. The strict discipline at Raja Yoga Academy had not been overly successful, either. He had been in almost continual rebellion there, had tried to run away twice, and once even tried to burn down one of the houses at the Academy. He was largely self-taught, and he had little difficulty in later years in applying the same methods to his offspring in the schoolless isolation of the Pacific.

In January 1920, after over a year of fitful work as a columnist and reporter for the Army's Marfa, Texas, *Saber* and the Fresno *Morning Republican* he felt he had saved enough money to start his new life. According to a newspaper story in the April 25, 1920, Oakland *Post Enquirer,* Robert's doctor told him he would not live if he stayed out the winter in the United States. Whatever the reasons for his sudden departure, which surprised both his friends and family, who felt he could not be serious about his plans to become a "South Sea beachcomber," it is safe to say it did not take much encouragement to launch him on his new life.

In *My Tahiti* he wrote of his thoughts before sailing: ". . . I close my eyes for the moment and forget the colorlessness of civilized life . . . and seem to hear even the distant mutter of the surf pounding along the barrier reef!

"An island attracts one strangely and inexplicably. . . . The charm may be engendered by the knowledge that here is something one might acquire in its entirety."

FJF

Contents

THE FRISBIES OF THE SOUTH SEAS

CHAPTER 1

Tahiti, 1920

A young man feels intensely the glamour of his first strange port, no matter how squalid it may be. But Papeete was not squalid in those days, nor is it now, though it has changed greatly since I first stepped ashore, young, alive to the picturesque and the unusual.

(MY TAHITI, page 7.)

Tahiti, in 1920, seemed at first to be the island paradise that Papa was yearning for. The principal port and main town of Papeete on boat day was alive with traders, sailors, natives from the country districts, fishermen, curious loafers, Tahitian girls dancing in bottle-littered bars, and "many Chinamen, like greasy fat spiders, behind their counters, bargaining shrewdly with equally shrewd natives."

The romance of being in a strange port for the first time fascinated Papa, and he felt that at last he was breaking into a land of adventure that was forbidden to all save a fortunate few.

As far as Papa was concerned, Samuel Wallis, who discovered Tahiti in 1767, might just as well have saved himself the trouble. Papa was out to discover it anew. There was nothing familiar; everything was new to him. He learned the ways of the natives and liked them. He sought the friendship of the white settlers, but preferred to live with the native Tahitians in the country. He later told me it seemed to him that every white man not in government employ claimed to be either a painter or a writer. The dry goods stores, the shoe-repair stands, the markets, and all things "practical" were left to the skilled hands of the Chinamen and Tahitians.

But when the steamer that had brought Papa sailed, he found that Papeete became overnight a quiet, almost peaceful village. The trading was finished until the next boat came, the natives had gone back to the country, the Chinese merchants had closed their shops. Only the Hotel Tiare, where he stayed, and a few bars remained open, and there the loafers, no longer curious, dozed in the drowzy air.

It was not long before Papa had made the acquaintance of the town's leading citizens, the schooner captains. He was drawn to these men of the sea, and listened with great interest to their stories of storms, pearl diving, and drinking. He entered easily into the life of the port, and thought that here at last was the existence he was looking for. He was twenty-four.

The knowledge that another young "writer" was in town did not surprise James Norman Hall, who lived on the outskirts of Papeete. Hall had noticed Papa on boat day as he stood on the dock, holding his typewriter and camera. At first sight Papa probably looked like an amateur traveler writer searching for romance. But later in the Tiare bar, when Hall met Papa, he discovered that this young nonconformist had *plans* for the future and truly wanted to write. Hall was in sympathy with Papa, who, like himself, had chosen the uncertain and difficult career of writing. He found that he and Papa held many a mutual idea.

"This is what I am looking for." Papa began one of the frequent long and serious conversations he was to have with Hall. "I want to make one of these beautiful islands my home. I want to live with the natives and know them inside out. I want to know them so well that I can write about their culture and their real way of thinking. You understand, Hall, don't you?"

"But, Robert, it takes six months out here before you find out about the acceptance or rejection of a manuscript," Hall answered. "What would you be doing for a living in the meantime?" Hall suspected that Papa could do with more money.

However Papa had ideas aplenty.

"I'll buy a little piece of land and plant coconut trees, alligator pears, vanilla beans, bananas, and then start a Noah's ark of goats, ducks, chickens, and pigs. Or I can take pictures of the pearl divers and copra makers and charge them fifty francs per picture. And since they'd have to have a copy for every relative, I'd really be rich!" Papa warmed to his subject. "Then there's O'Brien, who's writing *Mystic Atolls*. He asked me to do the illustrations, which could mean a little money. I already have a contract with *Leslie's Magazine* in the States to write short stories at seven cents a word. Do you realize that's the price of a beer for just one word! I don't think that I have much to worry about."

At first life in Tahiti was gay for Papa. He met many beautiful Polynesian women, but felt too adventuresome to settle down. He had no desire to marry and raise a family. He must travel and seek material. Already he had a germ of an idea that was to haunt him for all his years. He wanted to write a great sea novel he hoped would be equal to *Moby Dick*.

And keeping busy, Papa kept to his words. Within the same year he arrived in Tahiti he purchased a four-acre plantation in Papeari, about thirty miles around the coast from Papeete, costing about four thousand francs. There he built a well-

ventilated thatched house that stayed refreshingly cool even in the long afternoons. The roof of the house was made of woven palm fronds, and small bamboos, woven like a mat, made up the windows. The floor was simply a deep layer of gravel. The cookhouse was built about twenty-five yards away so that the smoke from the imu, or underground oven, would not enter the sleeping house and cause him discomfort while he wrote. He became such a devotee of the native-style house that for the rest of his life, on whichever island he lived, he rented or built at least one home patterned after his first at Papeari. Sometimes he would build three homes on one island, all quite similar in structure and architecture. This offered him escape when he was tired of one village or the noises of celebrations. He was free to gather a few books, his typewriter, and papers and walk to a more isolated house to continue his writing. Of course, often as not, he would join the celebrations, but he enjoyed the thought that he was not anchored to one spot.

Also, during this time he joined with two other literary-minded *popaas* (white men) to form the "South Seas News and Pictorial Syndicate." The "staff" consisted of Charles Brown, a successful writer for *Adventure* magazine, president; Charles H. Norris, business manager; and Papa, managing editor. They covered news of all the islands in the Society group. Since they had no competition, business was modestly good. In the meantime Papa took pictures for Underwood and Underwood and prolifically finished articles to send to the United States. The San Francisco *Chronicle* published, "When the Black Death Shook Papeete," "Will Politics Save the Polynesian Race?" and "An E Flat South Sea Island King." To the Fresno *Republican* went, "Last Cannibal Now Mormon Missionary," "Aspiring Young Men May Now Become Kings." He wrote two stories with the spine-chilling titles, "The Man-eared Serpent of Lake Vaihere," and "The Phantom Canoe of Moorea." These he sent to *The Saturday Evening Post*, but apparently *The Post* felt the stories a trifle "weird" for there is no record of their publication. In those days Papa thought these titles fantastically attractive and original. Perhaps they were "original," but in later years he was ashamed of them, calling them "amateurish and rotten"!

And he did find time to travel. He sailed to the Paumotu Islands and had his first experience with water spouts, which "came within ticklish closeness to the schooner." And while he was on Hikueru, a tidal wave swept the whole width and length of the island and chased Papa for the first time up into a coconut tree. Good experience to prepare him for the Suwarrow hurricane twenty years later, when he was to save his entire family from the waves. He dived for pearls with the natives and ate roasted dog during one of the many colorful feasts. He learned how to throw a spear at a distant fish and to converse with the natives in their singing tongue.

But in spite of all this activity Papa was not so busy or emotionally independent that he did not fall in love. He met a

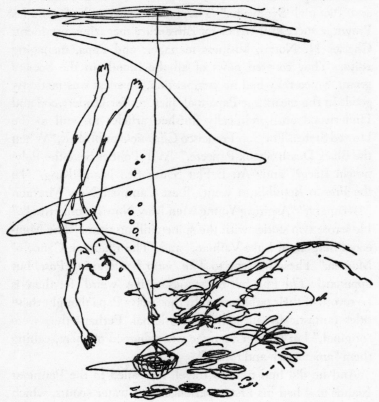

beautiful island girl called Terii, who seemed to be all he could want in a woman. Terii was a "Princess of the Royal Tahitian House," but this title was not rare since it merely signified royal blood traced back to the original Polynesian rulers of the islands, who had reigned before the French.

Terii and Papa were to live together for several years. "Do not be shocked, Mother dear, when I confess that Terii and I are not married." He exaggerated a bit perhaps when he continued. "There are no marriage ceremonies down here, and when a man and woman fall in love, they just consider that their love is sufficient without a piece of paper and priest's benediction."

Someday he wanted to take Terii to the States and show her the high Sierras, the only sight he claimed to miss. He wished to prove to his family that he had not married a savage, but rather a "beautiful olive brown skinned Polynesian, who has not been fed on ice cream and soda pop, whose hair has not suffered from curling processes, who has never used a tooth brush, nor seen a dentist and yet whose teeth are perfect and as white as pearls." But Papa was afraid of the reaction of his family toward his wife, and had rather Terii stay innocent of ugliness in the outside world.

After a year in Tahiti, Papa looked back on America as "not fit to live in because of its social condition." When his brother Charles suggested that he return to the United States because he thought the South Seas must by now be dull, Papa answered in a long and beautiful letter: "Is it dull? Where else would you learn that distance is measured by the number of pandanus cigarettes that are smoked in traversing it? So it is common to hear a man stating that it is twenty cigarettes to Papara. A cigarette, by the way, is smoked every kilometer, a kilometer is five-eighths of a mile so Papara is twelve miles from Papeete.

"Imagine me clothed in white duck sitting at the table of the Bougainville club with an island captain across the table, a South Sea trader to my right and a pearl buyer to the left. Let us have about three rum punches and the stories start—stories of strange lands and customs, hair-raising adventures, and even buried treasures. Then is it dull for the afternoon and far into the night?

"Or see me in a loin cloth and in my canoe, three or four miles out in the ocean. Let there be a fair sized sail, Terii, and a stiff breeze blowing, then let me come in towards the reef where the breakers plunge and bounce into the air fifty and sixty feet. Then when on the edge of a great breaker I am whirled over the reef and into the calm Tahiti lagoon, is it dull?

"Or take the best of them all—I am sitting comfortably in front of my bamboo palace reading a little, smoking a bit, and occasionally falling into a brief slumber. A coconut falls and I wonder if it would be better for a drinking nut or a milk nut. I hear the roaring of the reef-surf and watch some children, bathing, naked on the beach. A pretty native girl passes and greets me, and as is the custom asks me what I am doing. I tell her "nothing," and she passes on while I take a puff at my pipe, and returning to my book, perhaps read! 'There is a tear that no philosophy can dry and a pang that will rise when we approach the Gods.' That is enough to think about for the rest of the afternoon, so I drop my book and doze and think and doze again until Terii calls me to eat some *poipoi, miti haari,* and a cup of black island coffee. There is something about the tropics, brother, which you do not understand. There is a feeling of rest and comfort and contentment, which after all is one of the greatest things we can wish for, because after all what do we strive for in life if it is not a future chance for rest and comfort and contentment?

"And the points of interest. —I have secret information concerning two rich, uninhabited islands belonging to no country and only sighted once. Soon I shall go on an expedition with other adventuresome young men to formally discover these, hoist the American flag, and make a small fortune. In Rapa the women feed the men—in the Paumotu there is an island haunted by the spirits of thousands of big black dogs. They have been seen by hundreds. —On Danger Island the inhabitants bury themselves in the sand to sleep so the spirits will not bother them. —Three Spanish galleys loaded with gold bullion were wrecked and so far lost on the reef of Apataki. —The people of Huahine have a legend that Adam and Eve originated on a rock on their island. So they have human sacrifices to this day in honor of the first two inhabitants. —Oh hell, there are too many interesting things to mention. Please don't ever ask me again if I am bored in beautiful and mosquito infested Polynesia."

Papa's second love was a thirty-foot yawl called the *Motu-ovini*, which E. J. Spies, R. A. Sampson, and he had purchased and rebuilt in 1921 in the village of Papeari. Spies was another white settler—who had married an attractive Tahitian girl—and an expert sailor who, like Papa, yearned for the mast and adventure. Both were penniless. It was a rich and kindhearted man by the name of Smith who provided the capital to make the little craft seaworthy. Mr. Smith had great hope for Papa as a sea captain and astronomer. He provided the yacht with a fifty-dollar compass of the finest make, a one-ton casting of iron for the bottom of the keel, an Evinrude engine for the dinghy, and morale-boosting additions, such as brass portholes, brass-name letters, and a companionway door. Papa swore to his mother that he would never again expect to meet such a man as Smith. Smith made it possible for Spies and him to have one of the finest yachts afloat.

The announced motive of their trip was to explore the numerous islands and reefs near the equator that were not charted and had been sighted only once or twice from trading schooners. And if they ran into a nice little island they planned to establish a kingdom of their own and make laws to suit themselves.

They planned to cruise three thousand miles of the vast Pacific in fourteen months in their tiny boat. They were not afraid for, like most sailors of spar and canvas, they felt their boat was infinitely safer than a large steamer.

Papa, with the help of Mr. Smith, studied navigation and passed the test for his captain's certificate. He sent for his sextant in San Francisco, guarded by his uncle, Kirk Johnson. His mother and brother mailed him numerous books on navigation and astronomy, for he had developed a fierce thirst for knowledge of the sea and sky.

But trouble beset the adventurers even before they embarked. In the midst of their building the boat a slight grippe epidemic spread through the island, and all three men were forced to rest. They cursed the boat that had come from New Zealand, bringing the disease. Then, soon after recovery from the grippe, Smith contracted one of the most unpleasant of tropical diseases, elephantiasis. His legs became warty-hard and black in appearance, and remained in this state for the rest of his life. The only way to get relief from this disease is to visit a cold climate. However, the swelling will return as soon as the victim returns to the South Seas or any warm climate. But Smith stayed on to help with the fitful rebuilding of the yacht. It took over a year.

Another unfortunate delay occurred when Papa went fishing on the reef and stepped on an *onu,* a highly poisonous rock fish. He had to be under the doctor's care for two weeks. Fortunately, it was not very serious, although people often suffer severely and even die from the poison.

During these two weeks death became an obsession. Perhaps the dangerous long trip ahead frightened Papa. He asked his mother to help him overcome the fear of death that was haunting him to a point verging on insanity. "I seem to realize the material significance of it too clearly and I fear the end of my ego, my personality, which I unluckily love." He wondered now whether or not he would fulfill his desire to become a "pirate" with Spies, and to discover the mysterious uncharted Victoria Island. Papa's mood was not helped when Terii left him to marry a Tahitian boy.

In the meantime—during the long breaks enforced by lack of building materials or sickness—Papa and Hall collaborated on a handbook on the Polynesian language. There is no record of its publication. Papa also finished his first novel, called the *Tingley Book,* then threw it away because it was too morbid. But he never lost sight of their goal of embarking on "the great adventure." Still, it looked for a while as if they might never get the boat ready. By February 1923 they had put two thousand dollars into the craft and still had all their provisions and their sails to buy. At the end of that same month Papa's father wrote: "Did you take the little trip by boat that you were planning?" Papa was highly insulted, and wrote his brother: "Think of speaking of one of the greatest exploring adventures of the age in this tone. I have put my life and soul into this trip. For three months neither Spies nor I have tasted bread, sugar, eggs, or any wholesome foods. We are both as thin as we can safely be, because we have needed every cent for our trip. It has cost Spies and me just twelve dollars a month to live since we bought the yacht." His father further angered Papa by writing: "I trust you will be led to abandon that proposed sea voyage. I don't believe any good will come of it." (He also wrote that he was praying the trip would be frustrated.)

Finally, in July, they felt they were ready. The day they

were to launch the *Motuovini* they received a wireless that a gigantic tidal wave was rushing toward Tahiti and would half submerge the island. The excitement was intense. People threatened suicide, and businessmen started hauling their goods into the valleys, while most of the population fled to the hills and watched for a rising mountain of a wave to come crashing onto the island. Papa and Smith quickly consulted Bowditch and the Britannica on the subject of tides, made some calculations, and then sat on their veranda and laughed. According to the warning, the massive wave had originated off the coast of Chile. Calculating tidal-wave velocities, they had arrived at the conclusion that the wave would be exactly eighteen inches high when it reached the island. "Everyone else, Hall and the American consul included, feared the wave would be at least forty feet high when it reached Tahiti." Papa and Smith had a good laugh, as it turned out that there was a high tide at the appointed time, about twelve inches more than normal.

CHAPTER 2

The Yawl Motuovini

*I am deep in the mysteries of astronomy. I am nightly keeping
my house in its proper latitude and longitude by altitudes of
the stars, planets, moon and shooting stars, the only thing I
can't figure out is where the constellation Musca is. Your books
say it is in or near the head of Medusa, and my planisphere
shows it next door to the Southern constellation Centarii.
Which reminds me that it may be several months before I get
away, and so you will have plenty of time to send me your revolving planisphere if you still have it.*

(Letter from Papa to his brother, dated March 1923.)

The morning following the excitement of the tidal-wave
scare the *Motuovini* stood proudly under the French flag,
ready to sail. Her deck was like a vegetable stand, heaped with
bunches of green bananas, drinking coconuts, yams, and baskets of dried albacore and mantrap clams, and cases of rum.
There was also a crowd of Tahitians aboard who seemed determined to make the departure as lengthy and riotous as possible.

Among them were several pretty Tahitian girls of about

eighteen or nineteen years who had come to pour out their hearts to their departing *tanés* (boy friends) and to show off their new *pareus* (sarongs).

"Here Ropati-tané, take this *tiare Maori* [gardenia] and remember me always. You must not stay away long, for we shall soon tire of our Tahitian boy friends."

Spies sat in a corner with two sweethearts gently caressing his head and neck, each reminding him to return soon to continue their beautiful love. Sampson leaned indulgently against the mast, holding a tin cup full of rum and watching the scene with a broad grin.

The men bellowed and sang at the top of their happy voices, and drank rum straight from the bottles. Dancers, individually or in couples, would suddenly jump up among the crates to swish their hips to the rhythm of the guitars and the beating of the wooden *toeres*. Papa was giddy from the smell of the flower *leis* around his neck and the noise of the people. He was eager to leave. He wanted to yell, "Off you go!"

Finally an old Tahitian man, dressed in an undershirt and white, unpressed drill pants held up by a rope belt, gave the signal that the farewell party was over. Raising his arms and turning his face to the sky, he loudly prayed in an intoxicated voice, "Oh, Lord, these three foolish *popaas* have taken it upon themselves to sail this canoe to the distant lands. I predict that they will not go far. I ask You to follow them and return them safely to Tahiti for the benefit of many who will miss them. I thank You. Amen."

If it seems remarkable that Papa and his friends undertook a voyage of such magnitude, their success is even more astonishing.

They worked first through the most uninhabited smaller members of the Society Islands, and then after several months across to the Cook Islands, raising first the atoll of Manihiki, about nine hundred miles west and north of Tahiti. They certainly could not have expected the reception they received there.

The *Motuovini* was the second "overseas boat" ever to put into Manihiki during the lifetime of the inhabitants. The arrival caused, reported the Suva, Fiji, *Pacific Age,* "a great reception from the natives, who all assembled on the beach near the vessel, bringing presents of flowers, mats, etc., and performing dances for the edification of the plucky navigators."

Papa considered this an understatement. It was truly a wild reception. Half-naked natives went screaming to the beach to greet them, then hauled them off to their houses. All normal island activities stopped while barrels and kerosene cans of coconut bush beer were tapped and innumerable pigs and chickens killed. There were feasting, yelling, and drinking riots. Drums beat all through the night as torches planted in the sand lit the scene with an eerie glare.

The chief selected the most beautiful young women of Manihiki to keep Papa and his friends company at all times. The native men were complacent, knowing the white men would soon leave and probably never return.

As night gave way to day and day wore on again into night, the chief ordered more bush beer made of coconut milk or fermented breadfruit. Three days were allowed for aging. He also ordered the singers to sing the long-winded *himenes,* which are the history in song of Polynesia, and the drummers to beat constantly, particularly after sunset, when the crew of the *Motuovini* might be tempted to creep off to the bushes and sleep. This was a bigger riot than New Year's Eve or a wedding feast. And because it could go on as long as the visitors stayed, Papa, Spies, and Sampson soon felt they must leave or collapse from exhaustion.

When the Americans announced their intention of leaving

and brushed aside all invitations to stay longer, they were carried to their vessel shoulder high and all sorts of presents were bestowed upon them. It was sunset of the fourth day, and the crew felt unable to hold up under another night of merry-making.

After they had cast off, Manihiki was soon lost to sight in the fast-falling night, but for many hours, as they ran downwind, they could still distinctly hear the voices of the *himene* singers, the heavy booming of drums, and the piercing rat-tat-tatting of sticks on kerosene cans as the Manihikians continued the celebration far into the night.

They sailed northeast for about two hundred and fifty miles, sighting Tongareva (Penrhyn) at dusk of the third day. They had to drop anchor outside the entrance to the lagoon since the narrow opening would be too difficult to negotiate at night. But they could see the fires and torches of the natives ashore, in the village of Omoka, and felt quite cozy rocking in the offshore well.

Tongareva, like all atolls, was simply a slightly elevated, sandy portion of the reef that was oval-shaped and protected from the ocean swell by a deep lagoon, twelve miles long and six to eight miles wide. The reef was built up through the centuries on the remains of an ancient volcanic peak, which had eroded or sunk back into the sea. It followed roughly the lip of the ancient volcano, while the lagoon was formed by the extinct crater.

Papa wrote that they were well received on Penrhyn, and while a feast was held the first day they were given plenty of time during the remainder of their stay to rest and explore. The Penrhyn Islanders in 1923 were kind, jolly, and unspoiled. They made life very easy for their guests, and the visitors extended their stay to nearly a month.

But it was more than just hospitality that kept the *Motuovini* from continuing her trip. One afternoon in the sunlit depths of the lagoon Papa discovered a huge bed of mother-of-pearl. This was worth charting for future reference as pearl shell was much desired in the twenties. Certainly another delay was caused by the lovely Penrhyn Island girl called Teanua, with whom Papa fell in love. Spies and Sampson had found girls, too, but all three finally managed to get away, Papa promising to return after his trip to marry Teanua.

From Penrhyn the *Motuovini* sailed north, toward the equator, hoping to find the uncharted island known as "Victoria." The island had been reported seen many years before but had never been accurately located. No one had ever been on the island or taken its position, but it was suspected that "Victoria" lay about two hundred miles north of Penrhyn. After they had spent two weeks cruising the area, "Victoria" was still undiscovered, and the crew of the *Motuovini* set course for more certain prospects.

For the next few months they headed leisurely in the general direction of the southwest, with the Fiji Islands, some eighteen hundred miles away, as their eventual goal. On this course they visited uninhabited Suwarrow Atoll, where thousands of sea birds and turtles abound and where Papa was to meet his greatest challenge of courage nineteen years later. This island is about six hundred miles northeast of Samoa, and is reported to be the location of buried treasure.

It is true that in 1855 a certain Livingston Evans dug up a chest containing fifteen thousand dollars in coins and later a Tahitian sailor discovered another cache, of twenty-four hundred dollars, but the *Motuovini* was not so lucky. And there were not even any natives to throw a feast.

But the same, almost hysterical, welcome accorded them on Manihiki greeted them at the other numerous islands they touched, including American and Western (British) Samoa.

However, a month later, at the end of September 1923, at the conclusion of their yearlong trip, they were due for quite a letdown. As the Fiji *Pacific Age* put it, the Suva Harbor master, used to larger craft, "failed to see the tiny yawl sailing slowly into harbor, with the result that she did not get pratique till noon."

Having sailed thousands of miles, establishing what was undoubtedly a record for the Pacific for such a small pleasure boat, Papa, Spies, and Sampson were forced to sell the *Motuovini*. They could not live in Fiji without funds to await the passing of the hurricane season, which lasted until April of the following year. In a letter sent from Fiji to his brother Charles, Papa wrote: "It is a sad thing to part with a friend and that is how I feel about the *Motuovini*. The little ship is proud now, for she has sailed three thousand miles over the high seas and rode majestically through one ninety-mile gale. But soon she will bow her head with shame for her new owners will not treat her fairly. They will not carry full sail until she lays way over with her lee cabin ports under the plows through the sea at a ten-knot clip. They will not pat her slick topsides and praise her when she does well and forgive her when she takes on a sea. There will be some fat amateur yachting slob, who takes white women out for a Sunday sail, and who rushes to the halyards when the wind freshens and the ship exultantly lays on her beam ends and sails."

After a brief return to Tahiti, where he received the good news that his article, "Fei-Hunting in Polynesia," had been accepted by *Forum* magazine, Papa left his plantation at Papeari early in March 1924 and sailed with Andy Thomson on the schooner *Avarua* to Rarotonga, the capital island of the Cook group, some seven hundred miles southwest of Tahiti.

This was to be the start of a new and different adventure.

The A. B. Donald trading company on Rarotonga was interested in Papa's mother-of-pearl discovery the year before and made him an offer to buy pearls and shell for it on Penrhyn. This suited Papa fine since he planned to go there anyway to experiment on cultured pearls and see Teanua. He was to get a hundred dollars a month for his efforts, which would make him a wealthy man by island standards. And he felt he could continue his writing. So he sailed on the next schooner.

But on Penrhyn he could not find the solitude which he was growing more and more to love. And Teanua did not seem as enchanting as when they had first loved. She had a native boy friend and went off to see him each time Papa was busy. She was not a bad girl by Penrhyn standards, as girls, until they are married, are allowed considerable freedom of choice and change. But Papa felt she would find it hard to adjust to his life of increasing isolation. So he decided to leave Teanua and Penrhyn and for a long time only remember her.

By this time he was becoming unsure of himself as a writer and wanted to go to a place where he could concentrate on developing himself without having to worry about money and food. In a letter to his brother Charles he wrote: ". . . I am going to settle down to five years of solid work. My work will be writing. If at the end of this time it appears that I will ever be able to do anything better than mediocre work, then I will continue. If not, then I am free to quit and lead a life of ease. Frisbie's wandering and loafing days are over."

CHAPTER 3

Isolation, and Mama

A girl of about fourteen was sitting cross-legged, gazing into a
fire of coconut husks. She was naked save for the short girdle
of fern leaves about her waist, and her thick dark hair hung
loosely about her shoulders. Her skin, of that velvety texture
found only among Polynesian women, gave back the firelight
in soft gleams. Her slim brown body was as graceful as the stem
of a young coconut-palm, and light and shadow played over it
caressingly. She glanced up quickly at my approach and smiled,
unconscious of her nakedness. I smiled back—a foolish smile it
must have been—and hurried on, conscious of the hot blood
throbbing in my temples.

(THE BOOK OF PUKA-PUKA, page 38.)

Aⁿd so Papa found himself several days later standing
on the deck of the schooner *Tagua*, gazing with hungry eyes
at the approaching atoll of Puka-Puka. His job operating the
long-neglected trading store for the A. B. Donald company
would keep him in food and wouldn't take much time away
from writing. He was to be the first white man to settle on

Puka-Puka in fourteen years, and as he landed he must have remembered what the people on Penrhyn had said when he left: "Don't go! The boat only visits there every six months, or sometimes just once a year. You'll go crazy on that lonely, dull place." Perhaps this could happen, he thought, but at least he had found the most important thing he wanted: solitude.

Puka-Puka lies eleven degrees south of the equator, approximately four hundred miles northeast of the Samoa Islands and about three hundred and fifty miles due west of Manihiki. It

consists of a group of three small islets connected by broad barrier reefs enclosing a triangular lagoon about four miles long
and one to two miles wide. Walé, the main island on which
the natives live, is about one square mile. This pin point on the
map, sometimes known as Danger Island, is completely removed from the shipping lanes and, like many of the low islands
in the South Pacific, has no channels through the reef where a
ship could slip into the big lagoon. This perhaps was the fortunate reason why these islets were still unspoiled and almost
completely unvisited by white men. When Papa arrived, the
six hundred natives of Puka-Puka did little for a living. Copra
was all they needed to produce to earn enough to buy the
few goods from the "outside" they desired: a can of New Zealand corned beef, a dried twist of tobacco, or a calico dress.
Mother-of-pearl shell was plentiful in the lagoon, but the
Puka-Pukans had not been made aware of its value. And so
they lay under the coconut trees and slept, untroubled by desire for worldly goods or the need to labor for them. Time
seemed to stand still and calm, like the lagoon, and who really
cared whether this was 1924 or 1824?

It was into this atmosphere that Papa, with his trade goods
and books, was deposited, full of ambition but in complete
sympathy with the Puka-Pukan way of life.

Papa had little work to do, but instead of dozing the days
away kept conscientiously busy writing and reading volumi-
nously. He read at least twice every book that his mother and
brother sent him from California, and became frantic if the
schooner bringing a fresh supply was delayed. Still, he was
selective in what he wanted to read.

Once, when his brother sent him the wrong books, Papa in
disappointment thanked him in this manner: "Do you think
I'm still little Robert that you should decide what I am to read?
Not only do you refuse to send me what I order, but moreover

you and mother both advise me not to read Freud. Now, brother dear, you have bought a biography of Freud by Fritz Wittels and a treatise for children on Psychoanalysis. I am not the least interested in the life of Freud. However, I thank you for the two pamphlets by Freud. I read them last night and enjoyed them very much. . . . I look forward to a certain book for months, and then, lo, when it comes it's a substitute. You may be as peeved at the caustic tone of my letter as I am at the uninteresting tone of your books. P.S. Keep my checks coming!"

As the years crept by, Papa's library grew. It covered a space on the wall six feet eight inches high and eight feet long, and there were not more than a dozen modern novels in the lot. There were stacks of magazines sent from the States and Tahiti. His favorite magazine, the *American Mercury,* occupied much space. There were *Harper's, Atlantic, Forum, Scribner's, Digest, World's Work Golden, Geographic, Twentieth Century, Yale Review, London Mercury,* and dozens more.

And he found ample time to indulge in books he had always wanted to read. Eagerly he read *D'Artagnan Romances, The Three Musketeers, Twenty Years After, Vicomte de Bragelonne, Louise de la Vallière,* and the *Man in the Iron Mask.* He doted on a "lovely" edition of Conrad in twenty-four volumes, Swinburne in six volumes, and devoured the *Decameron* in four volumes. He eagerly read *Pepy's Diary, The Dance of Life,* by Havelock Ellis, *Tristam Shandy, Water Babies,* Spinoza in two volumes. With curious natives peeping in his door, he read aloud the poems of François Villon.

He studied each style thoroughly, and because he was intensely interested in the style rather than the narrative Papa had to read a book over and over to know the story. He wanted to thoroughly know each writer's style, so that his own writing would not read like Proust or Stevenson. Sometimes he walked the beach like a Buddhist monk, apart from the world. He concocted a special way of making tea to keep his mind alert and working at night. He awakened at five o'clock in the morning to swim in the nearby undisturbed lagoon, then walk the length of the island, here and there to sit under a coconut tree and read the *Memoirs of a Midget, The Beloved Vagabond* or *The Memoirs of Jacques Casanova.*

Perhaps no other white man then living in the South Sea Islands, except James Hall, read so many books and knew the English language as profoundly as Papa. People criticized him for using difficult words in his writing and when he spoke. Years later, when I was seventeen, a man asked me if Papa had used a thesaurus, and when I proudly nodded my head he laughed and in a mocking manner said, "So that's how he got by in his writing." This is the type of person who tries to pose difficult questions but is unable to absorb the answers he gets.

Papa often sat pawing over his books like a miser over his gold, fondling them, even kissing them. They were his greatest companions in the South Seas. Many years after, when the hurricane which I will tell you about later destroyed his library, Papa became a very, very sick man. He experienced grotesque nightmares, and we heard him screaming in the night the names of authors and the titles of books.

During his early years on Puka-Puka, Papa had to learn the most exacting patience. If he occasionally grew annoyed over the delay in book shipments, imagine the agony of suspense in having to wait a year or more to find out if an article or story he had submitted to an editor some seven thousand miles away had been accepted or rejected. And, often as not, the long vigil was rewarded with a rejection or suggested revisions. In the case of the latter, since the schooner was at the island for only a couple of days and during this time Papa was busy with his duties as trader, he would have to wait another six months before sending off the revised manuscript.

But all was not black. In May 1927, *Sunset* magazine published a humorous article on comfortable yachting in the tropics called, "Why I Enjoy Armchair Yachting." He got $125 for it, having been paid over three cents a word! This gave him new inspiration, and at a time when he was seriously thinking of giving up writing, feeling that he was a failure. He must have realized the absurdity of giving up such a necessary part of his life. He wrote an increasing abundance of material: books, articles, short stories, and poems. The *Atlantic Monthly* delighted him by publishing "At Home in Puka-Puka," *St. Nicholas* in 1929 sent him a check for "The Seas Afire," an anecdote about torch fishing for flying fish on Puka-Puka. In the same year the *Atlantic Monthly* published a series of four articles called, "Kanaka Voyage." Papa felt that the writing in this series was until then the best writing he had done.

But his happiest moment came in 1928 with the news that the Century Company was going to publish *The Book of Puka-Puka* the following year. This book is considered, by some people, a South Sea classic and the most accurate portrayal of life on an atoll, even though there *is* a whole chapter of fantasy in which native cowboys ride horses down the narrow streets of Puka-Puka. I suspect Papa was very homesick for cowboy land when he wrote *that* fairy tale chapter since there has never been an animal larger than a pig on the island.

Still, he was not completely happy: he did not think he had found success in his chosen field. He felt he must live a more exciting life in the lands of civilization, Tahiti or Rarotonga. The changeable climate and fresh foods would rouse his system. Conversations with educated men—actors, newspaper reporters, and editors—might help since those long periods with no one to converse with had made him self-centered. He felt he was beginning to sour on the world. This thought rambled on in his mind, and soon it was an obsession. Perhaps a wife would solve many of his mental and physical problems. He began to take more interest in his friendly conversations with Ngatokorua-a-Mataá, a lovely girl of fifteen whom he was watching make the sudden South Sea transformation into womanhood. You see, a Puka-Pukan girl is a mature woman long before she passes her teens, but still retains her childishness, a beautiful and precious jewel that no woman should shamefully hide.

Ngatokorua, within a few months, had blossomed into a gentle and beautiful woman whom Papa found himself greatly desiring as a wife. She was the fourth child of a native missionary who had sailed eight hundred miles in an outrigger canoe to bring the first Christian mission to Puka-Puka. It was shortly after the turn of the century, and the journey must really be considered a feat since he had no way of charting his course except by the sun and stars. His name was Mataá, and after he had established himself on the island he married Tala, my grandmother.

In English, Ngatokorua-a-Mataá means, "In Memory of the Two Who Died, of the Family of Mataá": these were two older sisters. In January 1929, Papa and Mama were married in a simple ceremony that took place on Yato Beach, on the leeward side of Puka-Puka. "Heathen" William, a friend of Papa's, officiated, and one of Mama's sisters was the only witness.

"Ngatokorua-a-Mataá, you promise in the name of the Good Man above that you will not sneak out to meet your good-for-nothing boy friends?" "Heathen" William began the wedding ceremony.

"No, I shan't do that," Mama whispered in her natural voice. "And I've never had *other* boy friends."

"You won't steal tobacco from your husband?"

"No!"

"That's too bad," Papa thought he heard "Heathen" William mumble. William loved tobacco, and felt Mama would be easier to borrow from in the future than Papa had been in the past.

"You will be a good wife to him, heh?"

"Yes. I shall try my best."

"Good! Okay then." He turned to Papa and continued, "Hold this Bible and answer my questions. Ropati-tané of Puka-Puka, will you take this woman as your true and *only* wife?"

"Absolutely!" Papa emphatically answered, kissing Mama on the cheek.

"Now will you promise me that you'll take care of little Nga, take her on your occasional trips to Rarotonga and Tahiti, help her with the children, and treat her better than the Puka-Pukans treat their women?"

"Yes. I shall take all of these husbandly responsibilities. Now will you give us a paper to sign and get this over with? Make sure you give it to the parson and calm him down a little."

Papa was sure the parson would be unhappy about being left out of the wedding.

"Here," he said, "give this twist of tobacco to Parson Kare Moana. And here's a twist for your pipe." Then he shook hands while holding Mama in his other arm. "Good-by, William. We are sailing away!"

And the newly married couple left for Motu Ko, four miles across the lagoon, to spend a week.

CHAPTER 4

Charles, Jakey, Elaine, Nga, and I

Little Nga has been in Papeete for two weeks, awaiting the moment when I shall be the father of a daughter. I want her there so she can go to the maternity hospital. There are a few good things about living in the South Seas. When she had her first baby in Rarotonga she went to the hospital and was charged nothing. This time I will pay about ten dollars for ten days' hospital. Altogether she will cost me twenty dollars, ten dollars for Nga in Papeete, and ten dollars for the hospital.

(Letter from Papa to his brother, dated June 1932.)

In June 1929, as the schooner *Tiare Taporo* on the horizon rolled dizzily, Mama's relatives began swarming around her house to weep and embrace her. Papa had decided to take his bride to Rarotonga and Tahiti and show her some of the world, and try at the same time to cure his depression. The Puka-Pukans fear departure nearly as much as they fear ghosts, and it can mean almost the end of a mother to see her child leave for another island. And so Mama's relations were not very happy with Papa for taking Mama away. They could not understand anyone wanting to leave beautiful, peaceful, and gay Puka-Puka. They reminded Mama that she would miss sailing to Motu Ko to fish on the reef at night and roasting young terns in the afternoons; or going to Motu Kotawa, Frigate Islet, to gather coconuts for copra, and sleeping on the white sand beaches.

"He is taking you to Rarotonga, a very faraway land, where the white men treat their women like slaves." (Rarotonga is some seven hundred miles south of Puka-Puka.)

"Ngatokorua, you are making a big mistake!"

But all this was selfishness, and it made Mama very unhappy. Papa almost canceled the trip, but he felt that Mama's sorrow would mellow in the passing of days, weeks, months, or even years. At present his health was more important. He feared he ran the risk of insanity by staying too long on Puka-Puka when he could easily regenerate by leaving for a short while. Papa, however, dreaded leaving the atoll. He was uncertain of civilization. His love of the simple and genuine had grown, and he wondered how he could stand living in the stuffy houses, with their hot corrugated tin roofs that glared in one's eyes, surrounded by burning pavement rather than the cool white pebble paths of Puka-Puka. And what of the noise? If the early-rising roosters bothered him with their noises, what might a buggy's wheel and horses' hoofs do? Or, horror, the steaming, chugging automobiles?

However, he found these fears groundless, and Rarotonga, population approximately two thousand, was still quite a peaceful place, although he felt people played their music too loud and he noticed that most of his friends entertained with the spinning gramophone.

Papa and Mama found a secluded house in Avarua surrounded by coconut trees that reminded them of Puka-Puka. They went for long hikes and camping-out trips in the mountains, which thrilled Mama since she had never before in her life been higher than the fourteen-foot elevation of Puka-Puka. But the mountains of Rarotonga are steep and difficult, and soon they had to discontinue their trips since Mama was with her first child.

During these happy times Papa still feared that he was losing touch with the world. He realized Rarotonga, although an important island in the South Seas, was still not civilization. He planned to take a trip home to California as soon as the child was born.

On June 23, 1930, Mama gave birth to a boy, and he was called Charles Mataá, after Uncle Charles in San Francisco and Mama's father. Soon after, Papa was on the sailing ship *Makura,* heading straight for San Francisco.

The journey was not successful from the viewpoint of a home-coming but it sharpened his wits and at the same time convinced him that the South Seas, and particularly Puka-Puka, was the best place a man could live. In a letter to his brother Charles, written on board ship sailing back to Rarotonga, Papa said: "It was depressing as hell being home. Except for the memory of you and one or two others, the whole stay in San Francisco seems like a fantastic dream—a wild nightmare of fat hangdog little men puffing as they try to work hard enough to please their raw-boned damned women."

During his stay Papa *did* have a little excitement. He took a brief berth aboard the three-masted schooner *Maréchal Foch* to Rum Row, an island four miles off the Mexican coast, as the ship was delivering rum from that island to San Francisco. I believe this was illegal in those days, but it gave him the material to write a story for the *American Mercury* called, "Rum Row."

Back in Rarotonga, Papa found his first-born had been

adopted by his grandaunt, Piki-Piki. Piki-Piki was a scheming but very likable scrounger who refused to give back Charles. This practice is not unusual in the Cook Islands, but Papa was apoplectic, and shouted and threatened her life.

Still, what could he do?

"Ropati, Ropati!" Mama soothed him. "I was very sick when Mataá was born. I could not give him my milk, so Piki-Piki adopted him. Everybody does that here, and we shall have another baby soon. Don't be mean to Piki-Piki, please!"

For many years after Papa and Mama had left Rarotonga, old hunchback Piki-Piki would hustle Charles Mataá into the taro patches the minute she heard news of a ship's arrival. She would hide in the mountains until the ship had left, or until she received news that Ropati Piritipi (her way of saying Robert Frisbie) had not paid a visit. This old Piki-Piki woman possessed the firm belief that Papa, or a sort of secret police sent by him, would someday kidnap her adopted son. Papa might have, but he stayed away from Rarotonga as often as he could, and when we settled there in 1943 Charles was a grown man who loved his grandaunt very much.

After a few months on Rarotonga, Papa was invited to form a partnership with J. A. Bunting, a former British naval officer, in a copra venture on Manuae Island, 124 miles northeast of Rarotonga. Papa needed money and had an idea copra might be more lucrative than writing, so he agreed to sail with Bunting and investigate.

Leaving Mama behind, he and Bunting, with eighteen Rarotongan laborers, led the lives of hermits, made copra, and planted new coconut trees.

The island was swarming with edible sea birds and sandpipers, and the lagoon and adjacent sea were fairly alive with fish. The men spent most of their time in or on the water, and it was a good life for Papa, but he found himself thinking

more of what a good story all this would make than of how
he might increase copra production. So after a few weeks he
sailed back to a happy Mama and wrote "A Copra Island" for
the *Atlantic.* Then away they sailed with Andy Thomson to
Tahiti.

Andy Thomson is a man with a reputation as a driver, and
with fear of neither God, the devil, nor death. As usual, Andy
wanted to get to Tahiti in a hurry. In fact, since the wind
was fair and blowing a full gale, he wanted to make a full run
and maybe set a record.

"Lord, brother!" Papa wrote Uncle Charles. "You dwellers
by the hearth can't realize what this sort of sailing means."

They sailed seven hundred miles in four days, averaging
nearly eight knots through a raging gale, with every stitch of
canvas on the ship. "Two sails were blown to ribbons and new
ones replaced. The schooner had only twelve tons of ballast.
She rode on the sea like a cork, and as the great seas heaved
under her counter she would lay over until half her deck was
under water and my heart was beating a tattoo on my ribs."

The sailors were paralyzed with fear, so only Andy and
Papa stood watch at the wheel. The first two days, Mama was
very seasick. She stayed in the cabin and ate nothing. But after
she courageously got up and peeked out the porthole to see
Papa smile in the wind she felt better. She felt much better,
however, two days later when the same porthole revealed the
outline of the green mountains of Tahiti.

In the early thirties in Tahiti five dollars a month for food
was quite luxurious, that is, if one lived in the mountains. Papa
and Mama lived with the Schumacher brothers in their two-
story house perched on a ledge on the side of a mountain. The
Schumachers also had a fine little garden and so much fruit
that it lay rotting on the ground. Mama immediately got busy
making mango chutney and guava jams, Papa showing her

how. Papa ate sliced alligator pears for breakfast, and then
alligator pears mashed and spread on home-baked bread for
lunch. Mama cooked breadfruit from the trees on hot coals
and poured hot coconut cream into the hollowed center of the
fruit, after first pulling out the hard core. This with a roasted
duck or a broiled hen was feast fit for even the French Governor
of Papeete. Many days Papa and Mama took horses and
explored the damp and rich valleys around them, eating ripe
guavas and mountain apples as they traveled. One day they
would ride to the foot of needle-like cliffs and the next to the
beach or bays to swim. Life was extraordinarily simple and
exquisite, and Papa's health was at its best. He began writing
My Tahiti, but it was not until 1936 that Little, Brown and
Company published it, because James Norman Hall did not
consider it good enough for publication earlier and he encouraged Papa to work some more to perfect the story. Along
with *My Tahiti*, Papa finished the unpublished autobiographical novels, *André Moreau* and *Teanua*.

During the years on Tahiti, Papa, who always suffered from
spells of pessimism concerning his writing, was greatly inspired
by renewed discussions with Hall. He wanted someone with
experience to criticize his work so that he would know the
truth about his ability. He found Hall's comments very con-
structive, and their talks were helpful to Papa's ego. Once
Hall read the manuscript *Teanua* and, finding a split infinitive
wrongly used, raved and tore his hair and told Papa that
perhaps he would be able to write in ten years' time. Later
he came to a scene describing Bully Hayes (a distant relative
of Teanua on Penrhyn Island) pacing the deck during a
hurricane, shaking his fists heavenward and cursing God, defy-
ing Him to do His damnedest, and Hall said, "This is he-man
stuff—so maybe you will make it in nine and a half years."
Papa was encouraged. He wanted this type of fair criticism.

Hall was helpful in many ways to the growing Frisbie family. When Mama decided it would not be long before she had her second child, Papa borrowed the necessary twenty dollars from his friend so that Mama could have the new baby in the Papeete hospital. Mama protested it as an unnecessary extravagance, but was probably secretly pleased when Papa insisted. And so it was that I was born within the protecting walls of a maternity ward, a convenience in childbirth that my mother was not to have again when the other children would arrive.

This was June 19, 1932, and that morning, while Mama was waiting, Papa was accomplishing a feat which gained him the high admiration of the natives. The reef outside Papeete is close to thirty yards wide and the sharp coral juts out of the water, causing the waves crashing over it to break and throw

spray from forty to sixty feet in the air. Riding the reef in a
canoe was common in some islands where there was not a wide
reef, but no one had ever dared do it in Tahiti. Papa was un-
aware of this and to take his mind off his expected fatherhood
he paddled his little canoe through the channel in the reef into
deep ocean, and then turned and calmly started to ride a
wave back over the reef. It must have been quite a surprising
thrill. The breaker that he caught fairly hurled his canoe
through the air. The spray dashed high above his head and
enveloped the fragile canoe in a blinding mist as he was flung
over the reef. Several natives were fishing in the lagoon and
saw the act. They immediately turned their canoes in his direction to offer help to the foolhardy Ropati in the remote hope
that he might survive the crossing in one piece. When the
white man in a rush of breaking water suddenly emerged and
appeared in the lagoon, darting between two jagged coral heads
at a speed of about forty miles an hour, they turned toward
shore to spread the news. And so when Papa arrived, there was
a mob of Polynesians and whites waiting for him with gesticulating arms and "incomprehensible" jabber. Only then did he
learn that it had never been done before, and that everyone
still considered it absolutely impossible. When he had decided
to go over the reef he thought that the natives did it often.

Of course, when Mama heard the news she was so shocked
and so very happy that Papa was alive I had no trouble in arriving.

Papa and Mama, with me wrapped in a *pareu* cloth, sailed
shortly after to the island of Moorea, twelve miles northwest of
Papeete, where Papa had decided to start a poultry business. At
least, he thought, we would not starve even if he was not making much of a living as a writer. And the chickens would augment the diet provided by nature. We settled at the head of
Paopao Bay. Most of the country was a jungle of lemon, hi-

biscus, banana, mango, alligator pear, and orange trees, too plentiful to be valued. "When one sees so much food rotting on the ground his appetite turns against it," Papa wrote his brother Charles.

This "Garden of Eden" was contained in a great rolling basin about ten miles across, surrounded by grotesquely beautiful peaks. Papa started out with twenty-two beautiful Plymouth rock fowls that grew fat in the mountains on bugs and worms and such things. Then Papa became fond of rabbits, and soon the homestead was overflowing with the furry creatures. To this collection were added goats, which provided my milk after Mama could no longer nurse me. We ate fruit from Papa's papaya grove and the banana trees that grew in the back of our house, and drank the juice and ate the meat of coconuts that lay abundantly scattered for miles around us. From what I have been told, we must have had a delightful life. We took our baths in the stream. Almost every day Mama buried my legs in the black lava sand so that I would grow up with straight legs. When Mama and Papa hiked to the near peak of a high mountain, I went along, too, hanging in a *pareu* cloth tied around Mama's neck. We did not have to carry food on these trips, as the shrimp in streams, the sprouted coconuts, and wild fruit provided sufficient snacks.

Life was not always this pleasant, however. Papa had recurrences of filarial fever (acute elephantiasis), and was in bed for days at a time. The fever left him with an enlarged leg, but the swelling soon went down under his special treatment, which consisted of wrapping the leg tightly with bicycle tubing sent over the channel from Papeete. In addition, we were penniless and in debt. Papa's letters to his mother and brother were written on the back of unwanted manuscripts. He sold his gun so he could sail to Papeete to see his friend Charles Nordhoff, with whom he was collaborating on a book, *Existence Doubtful.*

Work on this book often kept him up all night, and his writing was not at its best.

The book was about a soup tureen of pearls hidden on a primitive island. He wrote his brother of it: "Escaped convicts from the New Caledonia penal colony escape, capture a schooner, find pearls, and get wrecked on a hitherto undiscovered island. Then the *heros,* two young men, hear of the pearls and rediscover the island. There is plenty of plot and excitement there, but the principal thing is to show the reader what it was like on an island unknown to the whites. I imagine there will be no trouble about publishing it; all I'm worried about is speed." Unfortunately, Papa was wrong and the book was not published, nor am I sure whether Nordhoff and he finished it.

Sixteen months after I was born, Papa delivered Mama of my brother Jakey (William Hopkins Frisbie) amidst the cackling of the "plantation's" hens, the purring of rabbits, the buzzing of black mosquitoes, and the drunken yells and songs from the Tahitian neighbors. During the worst part of Mama's pains she looked at the steepled mountains of Moorea, where she could see the white terns flying in and out of their little bird caves, to forget how miserable it was at the end when the baby arrived. "But don't let that frighten you, Johnny," Mama later told me. "You forget every pain that you ever experienced and wish again to have another baby."

Oh! Mama wished that her next child would be born on Puka-Puka, among her relatives. But we did not have money, so we stayed on Moorea.

Then one fine day in January of 1934 a Mr. Starr (I don't know his first name or his homeland) approached Papa, asking that he sail Starr's twenty-foot yawl throughout the Cook Islands on a pleasure cruise.

"I have been told by numerous people that you are one of

the finest sailors in these parts." This was true. And Papa did not dispute the statement. He knew every inch of reef on most of the atolls and could sail from one island to another by the stars alone. After Starr left, Papa ran around the house, yelping and calling Mama's name. Papa was to sail the yawl all through the Cook Islands, and at the end of the journey Starr was to deposit us on Puka-Puka, nine hundred miles away.

Of course, when our friends heard of the trip, every attempt was made to talk us out of sailing on such a small, unseaworthy-looking boat, risking the lives of everyone on board. Papa's friends were particularly unhappy because Mama, Jakey, and I were also leaving on this journey. During this time of the year, from November to January, the weather was very unsettled, for the southeast trade winds stopped during these months and hurricane seas could be expected.

But only one thing bothered Papa. His elephantiasis. He would have to keep his leg bound and take large doses of quinine to keep the disease under control. Papa did not have money to buy quinine. He was so desperate to leave Tahiti, however, that he did not care about the attacks of filarial fever which occurred about once a month. Activities such as leaping, swimming, and climbing brought on attacks, so he had to be very, very careful. Among all the white men who had elephantiasis in the South Seas, Hall and Papa were the only two I know of who used preventive methods, looked to the future, and dreaded the thought of dragging a leg that might one day easily weigh thirty pounds. Keeping a leg bound with elastic bandages or bicycle tire tubes caused quite an unpleasant odor after a few days but did prevent it from swelling. (There have been cases where men allow the swelling to grow to the point where they must shamefully cut contact with society.)

One of the pleasanter stops during our trip on Starr's boat was on uninhabited Suwarrow, which Papa had visited on the

Motuovini. The island, about two hundred and fifty miles southeast of Puka-Puka, was owned by A. B. Donald, Ltd., and was green with thick groves of coconut trees and lanky pandanus trees that formed rings along the beach. Gigantic barringtonia and hernandia trees, black with gawking, noisy sea birds, were firmly planted along the spine of the narrow, long island. The dampish sandy beaches after sunset were playgrounds for the land and beach crabs roaming the shores—and in the morning before the playful waves washed ashore, inconceivably narrow footsteps marked the beaches, recording briefly the secret activity of the night.

Mama fed Jakey and me soft coconut meat, baked *utos* (an *uto* is the inside of a sprouted coconut, resembling the inside of a loaf of bread, but sweeter and spongier), and the orangy gooey fat of coconut crabs. I was only two years old and Jakey eight months. Papa wondered years later whether or not I remembered the noisy, wide-awake birds at night flying home from fishing. He laughed when he recalled how bossy I was, telling the wide-awake birds they were so noisy in the early evenings that I could not sleep.

We had been back on Puka-Puka less than a year when Elaine Metua Frisbie was born in Roto Village. I was only three years old but I correctly remember sitting in a corner of the trading store in Roto, watching our grandmother Tala and Papa help Mama with the birth of Elaine. I remember only two things about that year of 1935: November 29, the day Elaine was born, and a month earlier when Papa returned from another trip to the States. His three-week stay in San Francisco reaffirmed his *disillusionment* as far as civilization was concerned. "By no effort of the imagination will I ever again be able to consider that there are amenities to the life of the gregarious white man," Papa bitterly wrote Uncle Charles later.

The following year, 1936, saw Papa's fortunes improve.

My Tahiti, an autobiographical novel of his life on the island, was published by Little, Brown and Company. Then a series of three short stories based on his isolation-inspired hunger for wine, prime ribs au jus, and good black coffee was purchased by the *Atlantic* in that same profitable year. There were other articles published by the same magazine in 1937, the year Ngatokorua-i-Matauea was born. We called her Nga for short. I was five, and clearly remember Nga a few hours after she was born, rubbed with pungent coconut oil by our Puka-Pukan helper, Luisa. Nga did not mean much to me, for she looked like one of my oblong dried-coconut dolls. But I wanted desperately to go to Mama and kiss her and find out right away if I was still her favorite daughter. Later Nga turned out to be a pretty good troublemaker, and we made an excellent pair, fighting, racing canoes, and screaming, defending ourselves against Hardpan Jake and Elaine Metua. Our family was complete, three girls and a boy, small by Puka-Pukan standards but large enough, Papa thought. It was a good time for us. Papa was healthy and writing "like mad." At long last, some money was coming in from his efforts, and who would have been able at that time to predict that death would soon touch our happy family and change all our lives?

CHAPTER 5

The Church at Puka-Puka

Missionaries in the South Seas, brother, are a fizzle. The natives are much more Godly without them. The imbeciles come down here and first of all break down the old customs, thereby creating such ennui that the natives have to join the churches to pass the time. The missionaries forbid dancing and native himene *singing, and heathen rites, thereby leaving nothing for the natives to do for a pastime. Hence the church is the only outlet for their spare energy. Of course the damn missionaries are quite aware of the fact that they are forcing the natives into church by taking away all their amusement. . . . They have actually taught the natives sins so as to have something to forgive.*

(Letter from Papa to his brother, dated December 1925.)

Sunday on Puka-Puka is as beautiful and colorful as the island itself. We used to watch in fascination the religious ones marching like robots to church, careful not to take long strides for fear their starched white calico dresses or white drill pants might wrinkle, for most of the fun of going to church would be lost if they could not show off their Sunday finery. They not only walked from the three villages to the island's only church, but some also sailed their canoes across the four-mile lagoon, trusting in God to keep their Sunday clothes safe from the flying spray.

As far back as I can remember, Papa shied away from church, with the exception of V-J Day, after the war in 1945. But he believed in God. He read through the Bible many times and taught us the Twenty-third Psalm, and we would recite with him every night before going to bed. He did not like the Lord's Prayer, believing it consisted of many beggings. "We should not be beggers to God. I think He would prefer us to ask rather than beg for forgiveness."

Papa also believed one could worship God while alone in a room, naked or dressed. "A lot of people go to church to show their new dresses; some even go to worship. But people don't know that they can reach God anywhere. Go to church if you like, I have no objections. But don't be baptized now; do it later when you're older, when and if you decide to become a member of one church—when you are very sure."

"But what if we can't decide?" I once asked, a little afraid.

"Then don't join any church; after all, God is with everybody. If you believe sincerely in your prayers you need not go to church, and you need not worry about God ignoring you, for it isn't true that he would! That is not in his character."

In those days I did not believe Papa to be right in his religious ideas. I wanted to believe him yet I thought there must be someone who was making him think the way he did; perhaps one of the many book people he met in his nightly reading. So each Sunday we did not go to church I was afraid we were already slipping toward Satan's world.

Grandma Tala had told me many times that the Protestant Church was "God's church," and a Seventh-Day Adventist tried to convince me that her church was God's alone, and still a Catholic tried to prove by reading different passages from a catechism book that her church was the true one. How could I decide for myself when the grown people were not sure?

Elaine was baptized in Roto, Puka-Puka, where stands one of the daintiest little churches in existence. A yard covering fifty times the area of the building stretches before it like a rug, and a low white wall surrounds the yard like a necklace. Papa was away when Elaine was christened. The man who baptized her, without Papa's knowledge, thought the Puka-Pukans would consider him a hero for thus defeating his antagonist, the atheist Frisbie.

When Papa returned, nobody dared to tell him that Elaine had been baptized, and the pastor was particularly afraid of his wrath. He preferred to gloat in silence, knowing the whole island knew. If Papa had known, I'm sure he would have told the pastor of Puka-Puka to tear the page out of the registration book. This probably would have caused the recently "saved heathens" to think that Papa was a cruel man, a father who would rather have his daughter an enemy of God and burned endlessly by Satan than have her rise to heaven together with the rest of the good Christians.

But Papa seemed happy and even encouraged us when we dressed for church in our white frocks and Jakey donned his white pants and shirt.

CHAPTER 6

We Sail to Church

*. . . Contentment comes to a man during tranquil nights at
sea. The remembrance of storm-blown days grows dim. At such
times it is hard to realize that once the lazy swells were blown to
fierce combers; that the squall-flung spray had blinded,
drenched and numbed; that the fear of death had found a voice
in the wild screaming of the unabating gale.*

(Papa's letter to his brother, 1934.)

During the times we were living at Matauea Point on
Motu Ko we sailed Sunday mornings across the lagoon with
the trade wind. Papa was extra careful: he steered our canoe
well on these occasions, knowing that we liked to look our best
among other churchgoers.

At times when the weather was rough, Mama plaited little
square mats of coconut fronds to protect us from the heavy
rain. And when the weather was extra stormy, Mama stayed
home with Elaine and Nga, watching us wave good-by as we
zoomed, skipped, and bounced on the waves to Walé.

One Sunday not long after Potiki Nga was born, Papa,

Jakey, and I sailed to Walé from Matauea Point to attend church. Luckily, we did not yet have on our church clothes, for Mama wanted us to look our best and kept our beautiful white Sunday clothes in the storage trunk in Walé. These clothes were of white cotton prints, for silk, rayon, or taffeta was rare in the South Seas, and unheard of on tiny Puka-Puka. Papa was instructed to get them for us after we landed.

We were about one mile off the main island when the wind from the northeast unexpectedly blew its strongest, and in no time the boat had capsized and we were thrown overboard. The rain began pouring, obliterating our view of Walé. Jakey and I were close together, holding tight to the outrigger. Papa had pulled himself onto the turned-over bottom of the capsized canoe and was shouting instructions that the wind carried away.

A fine day that was to capsize! The waves seemed to reach the sky, and as the wind spread the foam in streaks I could see the "cat's paws" Papa had once described to us.

We drifted toward the reef for about half an hour, then, like a miracle granted us in the nick of time, Papa's bare feet touched an isolated coral head! Turning the canoe over with all the strength that was left in us, we started bailing. This took a long time, especially when all we had was one tin can that bent each time it was filled with water. Usually when a canoe capsizes and is filled with water, the Puka-Pukans bail by pushing it forward, then hastily pulling it back so that the water gathers and smashes against the end of the canoe, where it splashes out. It is a very good system. But since Papa was the only one standing, the canoe was too heavy and big for him alone to bail this way. But soon we were again Walé-bound in a canoe half submerged in the water, Jakey bailing while I looked for land, Papa strenuously paddling in the direction he thought the island lay. The mast and boom tied to the outrigger boom dragged in the water and slowed the pace. Then as quickly as it had descended the rain lifted, and there was Walé, a few hundred yards away.

As we came close to the beach, the Puka-Pukans, in their Sunday best, emerged from the coconut grove, waving and shouting excitedly, as if we were heroes coming home from war. They knew it was we, for they had seen our sail as we left Matauea Point just before the storm. The men helped Papa carry the canoe ashore, the women led Jakey and me to our house for a bath of fresh rain water from the village well and massaged us briskly with potent-smelling coconut oil. They should have done the same thing to Papa; he needed it more than we did. He was shivering, for all he had on was a *maro*, or what he used to jokingly call a French bathing suit.

When our blood was back to its normal circulation, Papa sent us to church while he looked over our home in Roto. That same afternoon, we sailed back to Matauea Point. The weather had calmed, but the waves stayed high; the breakers were still crashing on the reef, leaving long white sprays of foam in the air. What a sight!

From a long distance off we saw Mama with Nga on her lap, Elaine sitting on the beach, waiting anxiously. Elaine swam toward us, teasing, as if reprimanding. "You capsized, you did! I saw it!" Nga lay back on Mama's lap in a world of her own, not even realizing how excited Mama was. What a reunion! It seemed as if we had been away to church for six months and now had come home, weary but safe.

CHAPTER 7

We Lose Mama

I tried to take Nga back to Puka-Puka to see her children and her mother again, but these damn-fool medicos would not let her leave. They thought she might die on the way. What difference? She is going to die anyway. I will stay here in Apia till it is all over; then I will wander about until I get back to Puka-Puka some way or another. Anyway, with Jakey in Puka-Puka I will have all that is left of the family in one place where I can find them. . . . My news is that the treatment they tried on Nga—pnuemo-thorax . . . failed, because Nga was unable to stand it. Now there is no further hope for her recovery. It is just a matter of waiting. She is aware of this.

(Letter to Papa's mother, dated December 1938.)

Nineteen thirty-eight was a bad year for Papa. Mama became so ill with tuberculosis that Papa could not write. In August a British warship, the *Leith*, called at Puka-Puka; its next stop would be Apia, Samoa. This seemed a chance to get Mama away and save her life. Papa sent a radio message to the Governor at Rarotonga, and got permission to leave by the *Leith*, with Mama and one child, Jakey. Papa left us three with

the resident agent and sailed away to Samoa the very next day.
It was a sudden splitting of the family, and we were greatly
affected. Papa wrote to his mother: "It fair broke my heart to
leave the three little girls, and my heart is far from healed now.
I seem to think of them constantly with a sinking feeling, and
if I try to sleep I picture them in my mind, and then, oftener
than not, weep."

Even when the resident agent's wife cooked us rice, then
mixed it with sugar and canned milk, Elaine and I cried aloud,
for we wanted Mama instead to give us our food. Nga was too
young to care.

The doctor in Samoa treated Mama with a "new system
called pneumo-thorax, in which fluid is pumped into a cavity
inside the lung, thus compressing the lung until the patient
cannot breathe in it. This gives the lung a rest and a chance to
cure itself." After many months of this treatment the doctors in
Samoa told Papa that our mama would not live. The doctors
forbade Papa to take Mama back to Puka-Puka, but in spite of
this he managed. Some say he threatened to burn the hospital
if the doctors did not allow him to do it.

Papa built a new home for us in Ngake, where the wind was
fresh from the sea, which he hoped might cure Mama of her
bad sickness. But soon after we moved to our new home, Mama
died. It was January 1939.

I shall never forget the gentleness in Papa's face when Mama
died in his arms. Only the tears on his cheeks proved that he was
in great sorrow. I was standing in the doorway of our house,
staring at Papa, who was sitting against a pandanus post,
holding Mama. His head touched the post. He was looking at
the ceiling, not Mama. He began to cry softly, as if he were too
weak to really sob aloud. He shook his head slightly, in dis-
belief, and several times whispered Mama's name, caressing her
coconut-scented hair.

When he saw me standing there he waved me to his side.

"Your mama is dead, little Johnny," he whispered. "You'd better tell your relatives."

Outside of our house I leaned against the pandanus wall and cried and cried. Not only did I cry for Mama, but Papa's gentle sadness also made me very unhappy. When I told Jakey and Elaine, they ran home and started crying only when Papa told them himself.

Soon the neighbors, the relatives, and the whole island gathered around our house, some murmuring at Papa's selfishness in keeping our mother to himself. Others were wailing mournful sounds and chants. But after Papa had bathed and dressed Mama, the relatives took her to the mourning house of Ngake, we children trailing behind, allowing Papa to be alone. And we sat by her until our cook came to fetch us.

After Mama's death Puka-Puka held no inspiration or meaning for Papa. It was no longer beautiful and the ideal paradise for writing and bringing up children. But he was stuck. The schooner would not be back for months, and when it did return where would we go? As usual, we were penniless. So Papa kept busy by writing articles and teaching us our ABC's and European manners, in case we ever left the South Seas. But again he was not satisfied with his writing. He wanted his work to be so good the critics would rave about it.

"Yes, Hall," he wrote his friend, "soon I shall write the great *Hurricane*. Each day I live is an addition to my great book."

Papa also became philosophical and self-analytical, and wrote his mother such thoughts as: "Men suffer, and knowing they suffer, breed more men to suffer, and so the weary process revolves and the grave gulps them all the same as it gulped God, Buddha, Jesus Christ, and the man who cleaned out the pig pen."

His brooding grew even deeper as the days without Mama

lengthened into weeks and months. Again to his mother he wrote: "Sometimes I wonder what mental, or if you prefer, spiritual future is in store for me. Through hours and hours of meditation, I have lost faith in God, in immortality, in the divinity of man. I find myself asking: Is it possible that intelligent men still believe in all these medieval cantrips?

"The more I reflect on religion the more it is substantiated in my mind that men pray and believe in divinity only because of the fear of death. Sweep this fear away and with the same stroke religion crumbles upon itself. But what ambiguity! Even as I sit here in morbid ponderings, there comes the remembrance of vague mutterings from somewhere in the depth of me—mutterings apart from the vestiges of reiterated teachings in young life. What are they? God? Truth? The fear of death? Humbug? They are in the first nascent stage now and they will dissolve within themselves when I return to civilization and am confused by the babblings of a million pedants, but perhaps if I should stay on my island for a few years, wrapped in my own introspections, they would become palpable and I become blessed with mental felicity."

As the year passed, Papa also became confused about a more down-to-earth problem. Should he marry again? It was not good for him to be alone, but we children did not understand this and selfishly wanted to keep him all to ourselves. *We* did not need a new mother. When we had gotten over the shock of Mama's death we thought life was pretty good the way it was. We wanted to go on being spanked, taught, and put to sleep by Papa. He knew how we felt, and decided to postpone a decision. Besides, he was still too close to Mama, and no one, he felt, could ever really fill her place in his life.

That same year, Papa's third book, *Mr. Moonlight's Island,* was published by Farrar and Rinehart, in New York. The character Papa called Miss Tears in this book is Mama.

CHAPTER 8

Reminiscences of Mama

*I dreamed that I had wakened in a strange house and found
Desire seated at the table. She smiled and sipped her tea, but
did not speak; and she was dressed in the blue voile that became her so well. Her long hair was done up in European fash-
ion, with a wavy lock patted down on each temple, a tortoise-
shell comb, and a gardenia behind her ear. She was as I loved
to see her.*

(Papa's dream, THE ISLAND OF DESIRE, page 131.)

Mama was with us such a short time! All that I can remember of her are those things that cannot be forgotten. She
had the purest, kindest, and most beautiful heart of any woman
I have known. Most young people would probably say the same
of their mothers, and some would mean what they say, and
many more would say it only because it is a custom to say nice
things about one's parents. But no one could love a person more
than I did Mama.

Night after night Papa told us wonderful things about
her: what a perfect lady she was; how she cooked tasty Maori

food, swam like a fish, walked like a proud queen (but was not proud in her heart) and, what he thought most important, how intelligent and natural and unselfish she was. No wonder Papa loved her so much and nearly went insane when she died.

I remember her appearance vividly: her long wavy black hair and sparkling eyes, and her smallness. She was physically so small that she could not reach a green coconut from a young tree. And her smile seemed to reflect some secret happiness she was ready to share with all of us.

Mama used to scold me, softly, as if she were afraid I might crumble like an old clay statue. I often wonder whether she ever said a harsh word to anyone. Because she was extremely sensitive she was hurt easily. I shall never forget the only time Papa scolded her. And it was not her fault, but really his. The unhappy event was brought about by jealousy, one of those few bad habits of civilization still left in him.

It happened while we were living in Puka-Puka, on Matauea Point. That week was full of little adventures: hunting for periwinkles on the reef, sometimes eating them raw; stealing birds' eggs from well-knitted grass nests; and digging for sand crabs to use for fishing bait. Papa was over at the main island of Walé on business.

Every afternoon, Mama, Jakey, Elaine, and I visited Uncle Aumatangi, who lived about a mile away from our isolated house. We would all walk there through the narrow paths in the dark pandanus groves. Mama was always in front of us, clearing the way, picking up dried coconuts that lay in the path, pushing aside prickly pandanus leaves and dried coconut fronds. When the path became too thick with these obstructions, she carried little Elaine on her side and led us to the sandy beach, Jakey and I clutching her skirt, pulling on it as we stumbled on awkward feet.

Dear Mama! How much she thought of everyone except herself. She did not care whether her feet became ugly with scratches and cuts from the sharp, prickly pandanus leaves. Nor did she fuss because of our noisy complaints.

We would arrive at Uncle Aumatangi's little grass hut thirsty, and Mama would fetch us drinking coconuts, then take off our clothes and send us down to the lagoon, where she kept a watchful eye on us. And always she joined us later, placing us gently on her shoulders so we could dive off. Sometimes we hung onto her bare waist while she swam out where it was deep. Often when we wrapped our arms around her waist, Mama's flowing black hair in our faces gave us the feeling of being lost in seaweed as we followed her to the mysterious depths of the lagoon. Jakey, Elaine, and I could never have gone to the bottom of the lagoon when we were so young if she had not helped us. Late in the afternoon she took us home because Papa had told her that he wanted us there by sundown. She never disobeyed him.

Mama was not aware of it, but I used to watch her in admiring fascination as she gathered water from the underground well with an old kerosene can. Then she bathed us, one by one, in an old tin bathtub, and before we crawled under our mosquito nets she cleaned the dirt from our feet, her fingers searching between our little toes for grains of sand, tickling our feet. Then she told us folk tales, and recited beautiful chants of the stars, the moon, the sun, and the sea. We cuddled close to her, smelling the scented coconut oil on her body, the white gardenia in her hair, enjoying her very presence.

It was a wonderful week until Papa came back. He thought for some reason that Mama had been unfaithful to him and that at night she had gone off with her "Puka-Pukan boy friend." I did not hear the argument and I am so glad, for I would have felt miserable to see her face no longer happy. But I saw

her walk out of the house in her beautiful *pareu*, which Papa
had brought from Rarotonga, and disappear toward the village.
The three of us—Jakey, Elaine, and I—followed her, thinking
we were to be treated with a moonlight stroll, and wondered
why Papa did not accompany us. She turned and said to us
in her gentle voice, "Children, go back and stay with Papa.
Don't leave him." We watched her walk away and disappear
in the dark grove.

When we returned to the house we were startled by the look
in Papa's eyes—they looked as if he had just lost the most precious possession in the world. Why, he was actually crying,
not out loud, but tears were in his eyes and we could feel his
agony in the room as if it were something tangible.

It did not last long, this separation. The next morning, Papa
sent us to fetch Mama at Uncle Aumatangi's house. He knew
where she was. It seemed years since I had seen her last. I ran
to her with open arms, crying, "Mama, come home! Papa wants
you to."

CHAPTER 9

The Trading Store Makes Money

I nearly failed selling a native a pair of shoes because when he asked if they would squeak I ingenuously answered: "No, sir, I sell no squeaking shoes, my fine black pressed paper shoes are the kind that could be worn by any Brummell in the Opera." At that the native turned away in disgust, saying: "What good are your shoes if they don't squeak. I want squeaking shoes so when I go to church everybody will hear me and look at my nice new shoes. What's the use of shoes if everybody doesn't know you've got a pair. . . . Why, when I manage to buy such things as shoes I must notify the whole village of my property by resonant squawks and squeaks, as I walk down the village road." At that I brought out another pair of shoes, and guaranteed that they were the loudest squeakers made, being audible at eighty-four fathoms distance. I added a couple shillings for the extra squeaks, and made the sale. Next Sunday I saw him with his Derby hat, his necktie, and his shoes squeaking merrily as he walked to church.

(Letter from Papa to his brother, December 1938.)

From the house in Ngake we returned to the trading station in Roto, and Papa resumed his shopkeeping.

If Papa did not have his writing to burn up his energies and his reading to shorten the hours, I doubt that he would have stuck to his trading station for as long as he did. There is really so little to do as a trader in paradise. After a day without exchanging even a sixpence twist of dried tobacco or twelve matchsticks for a penny, I have heard Papa loudly complain to us children:

"Here's a day when I left the store open from morning till night, and no goddamn Puka-Pukan came to buy."

But he must have enjoyed trading because he made a game of selling the Puka-Pukans goods that they were planning to buy anyway—but at a later date. If a customer wanted only ten matchsticks, Papa would explain the possibility of strong winds that would use up six sticks all at once. And if the customer ran out of matches in two days, the store might not be open. So why not buy a whole box of matches, which would cost only sixpence?

The *Tiare Taporo,* as she had for many years, called every six months and left within two days, depending on how fast the copra was loaded. Immediately after she sailed, fading into the horizon, the natives turned their eyes back to land and Papa opened the store, allowing an eager, tightly packed crowd to swarm in. Very few of these wealthy Puka-Pukans had more than ten shillings to spend; some had none. And the penniless ones, psychologically, without their knowing it, helped Papa perform like a real trader.

One day when business was slow, Papa said to Jakey and me, "Kids, from now on I won't open any of the new smelly cosmetics [powder, soap, or hair oil], or fishhooks; but I shall pretend that the stuff I have in the store now is new. Just watch me fool old Tuapiko [Crooked Back]."

Tuapiko was passing by the store on his way to take a snooze in the palm grove.

"Tuapiko! My friend!" Papa called. "How are you? Come, I have three fresh twists of tobacco set aside especially for you. Here, come out of the sun and smell its freshness. It is so genuine it automatically makes you young. You are filled with new life the moment you smoke this particular twist. And your eyes will delight at its tremendous power to make you see well in the dark."

By this time Tuapiko was standing inside the door, still uncertain. Papa let loose his big thunderbolt.

"Your sweetheart will love this tobacco. It makes her weak and you strong. Kindly feel how moist it is." Papa carefully handed Tuapiko the tobacco. "And here is smelling hair oil—it is called Three Flowers, meaning there are three different kinds of flower scents in this one bottle. It comes all the way from an unknown land."

"E, Ropati, is this the oil white women use in those lands?"

"Yes, yes! That is why they smell so good. Your sweetheart will love you for this present. Here, I shall sell it to you for only one shilling and sixpence."

Soon Crooked Back was leaving for the coconut grove to smoke his tobacco and dream of nightfall, when he would overwhelm his girl friend's heart with the smell of tobacco and Three Flowers hair oil. When he was gone, Papa made a note under Tuapiko's name in the ledger. He knew that Tuapiko still had two shillings and sixpence left from the five shillings he had gotten for his copra sack the last time the schooner called. All the money the Puka-Pukans made was eventually returned to the trading station before the boat came back.

How Papa stood this sort of life for almost fifteen years, no one will ever know. But in 1939, after Mama died, he became tired of trading. He wanted to give it up and move from Roto into isolation on Yato. He selected a point of land which greets the wind from the sea, and from which we could just barely see our old home in Roto.

He gathered the Puka-Pukan high officials to make arrangements for men and women to help him build our house, in return for a supply of tobacco, some rice, flour, and lots of corned beef and some kerosene.

A month later we packed our belongings, Papa's writing materials and books, and walked the half mile to our new home.

CHAPTER 10

The House at Yato

My house is beautiful. There is no garish paint to distress the eye. The pandanus framework, the wattling, and the mats are the color of new-mown hay; the blinds and the thatching are russet brown; mats are on the triclinium couches and tables and the shelves where I keep lamps and books and such things. There are dashes of red in the mat design—just enough to break the monotony. Patches of pure-white coral gravel show here and there on the floor; and, to set off the whole scheme, there is, to the east, a view of the azure-blue bay, with the Point of Utupoa and the Central Village houses a half mile away.

(THE ISLAND OF DESIRE, page 91.)

If I were granted a wish I would ask for a house like our third and last home on Puka-Puka, the one at Yato. The construction of that memorable house was perfect. It was built almost completely of pandanus, a tall, branching tree of soft wood, covered by thick, hard, polished bark and many clumps of long, shiny, brilliantly green leaves. It was erected on a flat

mound of clean white gravel, which served as the floor. Thick
pandanus trunks made the four main supporting posts. *Tou*
(cordia) wood was used for the crossbeams. Split, dried
pandanus roots formed the wall, while the roof was fashioned
of plaited pandanus leaves. All these elements were joined
and held together by strong bonds of coconut sennit.

Papa built a little room in a corner where he could work.
It was on the windward side, where the soft breeze from the
lagoon triumphantly swept away the pestering mosquitoes.
In the living room we put up bunks of pandanus root along
the walls of the house, stretching in a U along three sides of the
room. They were made low to the floor, level with the single
long window that encircled the room. It was like sleeping out-
doors when the coconut-leaf shutters were pulled to the ceiling,
almost touching the overhanging thatched pandanus roof.
We could look out and see the nearby coral beds when the tide
was low, and far across the lagoon the native villages of Roto
and Utupoa. We smelled the fresh salt water, the moist,
luminous sand at night, the pleasantly scented pandanus
blossoms on the seashore. We heard the lazy waves gently
folding and rolling on the beach. But, most of all, I remember
being greeted through the window early in the morning by the
fishermen going out to sea, their paddles humming as they
pulled through the still water.

And on each bunk there was a beautifully plaited thick
moenga (mat), and a *pareu* quilt neatly laid on each kapok
pillow. They were the same pillows we had carried with us to
every island we had visited. During nights when the coconut
and pandanus leaves rattled and scratched against the roof,
the wind carried salt spray to our faces from the lagoon. We
had a habit some mornings of licking the fresh salt from the
smooth pandanus posts. If the lagoon was still, we slipped over
to the windward side of the house, leaving wrinkled *pareus*

on our bunks, to dive into the beckoning water only ten feet away. It was never chilly, so we didn't have to test it with our toes before jumping in.

The gravel floor was made of fresh white pebbles, polished smooth and rolled to our door by the waves. We did not sweep, we "raked" the floor to keep it clean and neat. Often during the mosquito season we used the big living room as a bedroom since there were no chairs or tables to move aside. The mosquito net covered the entire room: the four ends of a big piece of netting were tied to the four polished posts, one built in each corner of the room.

Many nights after Papa had told us of Ulysses and his travels, of Paris and Helen, or the nymph Calypso, and had given us a bumpy ride on his bony knees, explaining that this was how he used to ride the horses in cowboy land, we would crawl happily under the net. The net gave us the impression that we were going to bed in a world set apart just for us. In it we fought, giggled, and screamed like happy animals.

Almost every night, Elaine had the good fortune to sleep beside Papa, for she was not as skinny as we were. Her soft, fat legs, her well-padded bones could not hurt him when she turned and kicked in the night. Her chubby little arm was as light as a kitten upon his chest. However, Jakey, Nga, and I were too bony, for if we slept near Papa every time we turned or even moved we thrust our sharp knees into his side, arousing his sleepy anger. How we regretted being skinny!

Papa knew quite well that sleeping by his side meant much to us. Sometimes he allowed Jakey to sleep beside him with the understanding that Elaine could sleep there the following night so that Papa could catch up on his sleep. When my long-awaited turn came, Elaine again would be the fortunate one the following night. She was a lucky girl.

In the mornings, whoever had slept beside Papa told the

other children an often repeated story: "You know something, I didn't even sleep a wink last night. I was so afraid that if I kicked Papa in my sleep he would send me away. And there was a time when I wanted so much to scratch my head—you know how it is—good thing I didn't, though, or Papa would have found out the lice in my hair."

CHAPTER 11

A Quiet Night

News from the islands! Just this moment I lifted my eyes to glance at a lizard egg on a shelf above my typewriter. I had nine there, but only two were left, for the others had hatched. As I glanced the egg broke to pieces and a little lizard jumped out, ran along the shelf and jumped onto the window screening. It all happened so quickly that it fairly took my breath away. The lizard ran up the screening, and within ten seconds of the time he had hatched caught a fly and swallowed it. That little fellow did not need any training. Who can explain this? Was the nascent intelligence in the embryo, or is there a group mind affecting all lizards?

(Papa's letter to his mother, 1934.)

Often as I lay awake at night, unable to sleep, such a confusion of questions would come to my mind that I wanted to wake Papa there and then and talk. There were questions about mysterious America, gentle Mama, how I could learn to type with two fingers, how to write stories, how to change the typewriter ribbon, read rapidly, how to ride a horse, and questions about different girls Papa was seeing. But I very seldom asked questions, for Papa's thoughts seemed far away and the meanest thing we could do was to disturb him while he was deep in thought or working. Even when he was asleep, we believed he was dreaming of his writing.

One night when I was about eight years old, after a tasty dinner of smelly raw fish, baked bananas, and sour coconut cream, we retired early into our little world beneath the mosquito net. I had not slept by Papa's side for many nights, and felt unloved. I stayed awake, childishly trying to analyze the reason, when I found myself wiping the tears with the back of my hands. I did not want to be heard sobbing so I crept slowly and noiselessly out of the net.

I walked a little way to the beach, too afraid of ghosts to wander far, and sat on the undisturbed cool white sand. I watched the lagoon, the shadows of the coconut trees visible in the lucid water, their fronds slowly moving back and forth, as if dancing the Hawaiian hula to the music of the soft easterly wind. Across the small bay I saw lights glimmering, but I could not see the roofs above them so I pretended they were stars. Sand crabs crawled out of their holes beside me. Funny how sand crabs live, I thought. They work very hard at night, digging and clearing holes, then early in the morning they scamper into the shallow water to wash their shells quickly and crawl back into their comfortable damp holes, being certain to cover themselves with sand so they can sleep peacefully all day. Some people live that way, too, I thought. They work all night and sleep all day. Look at Papa—I've known him to write all through the night, until the lantern has run out of kerosene, and sleep all the next day.

I had the strange feeling suddenly that somebody was nearby, watching me. I felt the hairs on my arms prickle. I waited a long time before I turned my head to the left, toward the westward side of the island but the crabs were still busily working. The same was true when I looked eastward. I glanced at the water, but the little silvery *kalomas* (silver mullets) were peacefully sleeping on the sand in the shallows. Then I slowly turned and saw the dark blue silhouettes of the coconut fronds, while above my head were *kakas* (white terns), nesting in pairs. *They* are staring at me, I thought. I guess they are afraid that I might throw a rock at them, as Brother Jakey sometimes does.

Then, crawling quietly from nowhere, like a thief in the night, a rat appeared on the branch, not far from the terns, looked at me curiously, with his whiskers twitching, hopped a little toward the birds, cast another mean look at me, then decided it was not worth the trouble to attack. I saw his long, stringy tail quickly disappear into his nest in the heart of the coconut tree, where he undoubtedly told his family of the danger he had just escaped.

I felt better. I did not think life was so bad after all, and I did not care so much whether or not Papa loved me. At least my night friends noticed me. And the moon above, smiling down, was only for me! I smiled back at her and asked that she not fade away until early dawn.

I finally fell asleep on the sand. When something awakened me, I thought it was just the heavy salted air that pressed against my cheek. Soon I detected someone breathing, and knew at once who it was. My little brother gently lifted my head onto his arm, and after a while whispered, "I looked all over the place for you."

"You go on back inside before Papa finds out we're here!" I tried to be stern, pushing him a little.

"You come, too. He's going to be angry with you, and then scold me for not watching you. Come on, let's go!"

I went back without an argument. Jakey and I were very

close, and often did things to make each other happy. We would fish together, trap birds, and dive for pearls or for the rare white clay which is found only in the deepest part of the lagoon. He used to build boats and canoes out of tins and odd pieces of driftwood; little tree houses and bird cages—all for me.

We crawled back to bed noiselessly, said a little prayer, then closed our eyes.

The next morning at breakfast Papa asked, "Did someone go out last night?"

Jakey and I looked at each other and smiled guiltily.

"Maybe there's a hole in the mosquito net. We had better find out. There were mosquitoes inside the net, and I want to know if one of you went out without tucking the net back under the mat."

He looked at the ceiling and blew a smoke ring. "From now on make sure that every single one of you tucks the net under the mat when you go out: whether to swim, to sleep on the beach, or visit the w.c., understand? That doesn't mean you can sleep out every night. Absolutely not!"

"Yes, Papa!" Three answers came at once.

"You, Potiki, did you hear what I just said?"

"Yes, Papa," Nga answered, pinching me on the knee to repeat Papa's instruction.

"What did I say?" he asked again, a little smile betraying his good humor.

"The mosquitoes bit you last night?"

"Well, you're pretty close."

Papa looked around toward the lagoon. For several minutes he seemed to study it with the utmost concentration, while we watched quietly. Was he thinking of taking us for a canoe ride or maybe a long swim? Or maybe he was considering

taking us all fishing. Then suddenly turning with a faraway
look still in his eyes Papa stated, "I'm going to write now. I'll
have lots of typing for you to do tomorrow."

Damn that beautiful lagoon!

CHAPTER 12

A Moonlight Night

*For in the quiet hours of night, while lying on our sleeping
mat, only vaguely conscious of the snores of the Watch and
Ward out woman-chasing in their dreams—while longing once
again to drink tea and read Browning with Penelope—while
pondering chastity, purity in thought and deed, suppression
of the bestial cravings of the lower man—how often do we
hear the crunch of coral gravel under bare feet, a soft inconti-
nent laugh, husky girl voices whispering! The stairs creak;
the folds of the mosquito net ripple; the odor of scented coconut oil insinuates itself into our thoughts as welcomely as the
fingers, the lips, the breasts of an atoll Calypso hungry for love.*
(THE ISLAND OF DESIRE, page 49.)

O n the atolls in the South Pacific sleep often came soon after sunset. Of course, there were those full-moon nights when
sleep seemed unthinkable. Those maddening and hair-pulling
nights when that great yellow moon rose slowly from the
coconut trees, clearing a path through the palm fronds and
casting a light so bright that night was magically turned into
silver day. Sleep was far away on those nights.

But it was still harder to go to sleep when the whispering voices of the young people playing atoll night games came to our ears. Curfew for them was a law to be gleefully ignored if mentioned by cross parents. But with Papa there was a set time at night for "the cowboys" to be in the house. We used to lie in bed, one ear to the open window, trying to identify the boys by their familiar voices and the young women by their giggles. If we looked out the window we could see silhouettes of half-naked boys and girls sneaking among the bare trunks of the coconut trees.

On our hard wooden beds we twisted our toes and bit our lips, wishing that Papa would say, "Why don't you kids join the games?" He never did. But one white night the call of adventure overcame all of Papa's warnings as I lay listening to the alluring sounds of laughter and splashing water. Temptation was too great! Crawling out of bed, careful not to disturb the others, I carefully tiptoed out of the house, across the rustling pebble bed that surrounded our home. Reaching the coconut trees, I ran like a scared cat to the fun that was waiting.

A few minutes later, of course, Jakey joined me. The guilty expression on his face was soon replaced by excitement.

"I knew you weren't going to the w.c.," he stated.

I looked at my little brother and laughed, "Jakey, do you always have to wait for me to leave first?"

Everyone was gathered on the beach, organizing a game of hide-and-go-seek. Soon the boys disappeared down a narrow path, halfway inland, where it was dark, and the girls set about finding suitable hiding places.

Now Puka-Pukan girls are not very ladylike when it comes to having fun. For a hiding place a girl might crawl under a dried frond and lie on her back. Of course, this meant lying still among the lazy lizards, ambitious ants, and bubbling land crabs, who displayed some annoyance with the bothersome invader. If she made the slightest movement, the rattling leaves would reveal her presence.

Sometimes a girl would look for the thickest grove of maire ferns, crawling instead of walking into the grove so as not to leave a trail. When these ferns were disturbed, the orange-colored pollen brushed against the face, causing an almost uncontrollable desire to sneeze. This added to the excitement! Some girls even covered themselves with heaps of dried oblong coconuts. Others squeezed into the twisted labyrinth of lanky pandanus tree roots, frightening a few hermit crabs in the process. A few more ambitious girls covered themselves with sand, their noses alone exposed to sniff the fishy smell from the sea.

Cousin Tili and I took off our clothes and stood close to a coconut tree, for the color of our skin blended well with the trunks in the dark. This was fun, because we saw everything that was going on: the boys discovering the girls and chasing them into the sea, laughing as the girls willingly and shamelessly undressed.

The boys had more fun, we thought. We also accused them of being unfair in picking their hiding places. For instance, they might swim a hundred yards out into the lagoon to sit on coral heads, low and dark against the water. Or they often climbed the tallest trees to sit, suppressing their laughter as they watched us running about like fools below them. They even invaded people's homes to crouch on the crossbeams in the ceilings, or to lie flat on the thatched roofs.

This game lasted until midnight. Then we all took off our clothes, without shame, threw them carelessly on the beach, and with loud screams ran into the water, shivering with pleasure as the fresh ocean washed the salt from our bodies.

CHAPTER 13

The Pig Hunt

*I am no sportsman, nor have I any sympathy for the sportsman's
code. . . . I tell my huntsman friends that their idea of
sportsmanship implies a vicious desire to kill. It thrills them to
wing a bird and see it die. Many of them kill a dozen birds, on
the wing, in the authorized manner, with the authorized
weapon, but only for the pleasure of killing, for rarely do they
need so much meat . . . and so long as one kills for food one
may as well admit himself a barbarian, no matter how the killing is done.*

(MY TAHITI, page 131.)

Papa had the habit of taking walks: with long strides he
traversed the gravel paths connecting the three villages of
Puka-Puka, often gesticulating as he conversed with himself.
On certain days Jakey and I would trail him from Yato,
through Roto, to Ngake, then back to Yato. We held his
tanned, hairy hand when possible, but most times we kept some
distance behind because he wanted to be left alone.

One day we discovered he had a mission. Having decided

to replenish our larder, he was out to find and butcher the biggest and fattest pig on the island.

Pigstys on Puka-Puka were built of coconut trunks laid out in squares, one on top of the other until they reached a possible height of ten feet. There in those prison-like cubicles the hairy creatures lived and were fed, not with leftover food, but with fresh coconut meat and sweet coconut milk. This was true only on Puka-Puka, whereas on Manihiki, Penrhyn, and Rarotonga pigs were fed with leftover food, like fish, taro, or even pig's fat.

It took four hours before Papa found the right pig, fat and round like a young coconut.

"He'll fill *three* kerosene tins with drippings!" Papa exclaimed excitedly to us.

And very early the next day curious and whispering Puka-Pukans came from their villages, drawn by the prospect of something unusual. For it was only once or twice a year that Papa, "the white man," shopped for a well-fed pig.

From under the shady coconut and hernandia trees came naked brown children, leaving behind their marbles. Women hurriedly covered umus with wet coconut husks and copra sacks, bending over the oven as they did, their sweat sizzling on the hot rocks, smoke covering their faces. And the men roused themselves from their morning snoozes, finding it impossible to sleep through the excitement. The women took to chatting and gossiping over the screams of children and the rattling of the coconut fronds as they plaited baskets, waiting for Papa to come out of his writing studio. Then, as if sensing the dramatic moment, he stepped out into the sunlight, clad in a white *maro*, a faint smile on his face.

He walked to the pigsty, five husky Puka-Pukans following him to help drag the grunting, protesting pig to the beach. There the women had already prepared torches from dried coconut fronds and finished weaving baskets of green coconut leaves to hold their share of the pig's insides. ("What would the people of Puka-Puka do without the coconut trees?" Papa once asked a Puka-Pukan. The Puka-Pukans very seldom think deeply when asked a simple question. "What do you mean 'without' the coconut tree? We *have* coconuts don't we, Ropati?")

Papa weighed the pig and recorded in a black notebook its weight and size. Proudly Jakey handed him the recently sharpened knife for the big moment that was to follow. Four very strong Puka-Pukans, muscles rolling, firmly held the pig's legs. Its jaws had already been tied with a rope so that its soprano scream would not drive Papa to madness. He hated sharp and penetrating noises.

Placing one of his bony knees on the pig's hairy and wiggling stomach, the other in a crab hole for firm support, he carefully removed the knife from his mouth, pointed it at the pig's tender neck, right below the left ear, and quickly thrust it home. As the blood gushed out, the women covered their faces with their hands. Young children screamed and scrambled in frenzy toward their mamas, while the men looked at them with annoyance. Even Jakey glanced at me disapprovingly as I looked away in horror.

The blood stopped almost as quickly as it had begun. I am not bragging when I say that nobody but Papa could kill a pig as fast and with less loss of blood, for usually the knife is pushed in and pulled out of a pig's neck so many times that before the pig finally dies, half its blood is wasted. That was why during Christmas holidays, or any other big celebration, we watched Papa sharpen his precious and only knife in preparation for the kill. In return for this service the Puka-Pukans would present him with a whole pig, alive or cooked.

Or sometimes they would help build us a new thatched-roof house.

Now as the pig lay lifeless, the women peeped through the gaps between their fingers; the children, after comforting words from their mothers, joined little gatherings of excited play-mates. The men lit the torches and burned the pig's hair. Another group of men scraped the burned hair off with well-sharpened knives. At the end of this process the pig was no longer dirty and black and hairy. It looked clean and white, as if wrapped in a sheet. Then Papa dipped his hands in a bucket of clean salt water and washed it down. He did not believe in scrubbing a pig with soap or sand, as the Penrhyn Islanders do, and the Puka-Pukans thought his system was best.

Papa and his helpers worked smoothly and without wasted motion. He slid the knife down the length of the pig's stomach and pulled out the intestines, guts, heart, and liver, and the men put the separate parts into waiting baskets. Finally when the pig was completely emptied, like a *paté* (hollow music log), Papa stuck his head inside its stomach to give the Puka-Pukans a little thrill that would keep them happy and talking for the rest of the day.

"*E mea umere* [How amazing]!" they murmured with pride.

The pig was then cut into little pieces and dumped into the iron boilers in our cookhouse. After the butchering all the people started for their homes, talking and pantomiming the way Papa had held the sharp knife between his teeth, stabbed it into the pig's neck, and killed the beast in so short a time. Even the next day they still talked about it.

The meat lasted many, many weeks, because the cooked pieces settled at the bottom of the boilers, the fat covering the meat. In this way it was preserved for a long time. For months we ate pork, pork, and more pork, until *we* felt like pigs.

CHAPTER 14

Panikiniki

Calm and variable winds. How many tens of thousands of master mariners under sail have made that entry, but how little it means to a landsman or even to a steamship sailor.

(DAWN SAILS NORTH, page 253.)

On Christmas of 1941, when I was nine, the people of Yato Village presented to us a beautiful canoe built from the trunk of a giant hernandia tree. We later named her *Panikiniki*, which means "Skipping," because of her ability to skim over coral beds when sailing fast with the wind.

But owning a canoe at first presented a problem. We had no sail, and had to wait long, anxious months for the schooner to bring the sailcloth we had ordered. Papa spent the time profitably, teaching us children how to sew with practice cloth and sail needle, so when the material finally arrived he had a talented if overeager crew, ready to produce the finest sail in the South Seas.

Papa handled that cloth like a mother holding a newborn babe. He kept the sail inside the house, spreading it out and

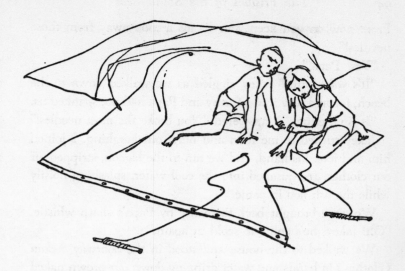

sometimes becoming lost in it, like a busy crab on a shifting white beach.

"Clean your feet before you enter!" Papa automatically ordered when he saw us coming into the house, half of him wrapped up in the canvas.

He reluctantly let us help him, for he felt it best we take part in the work even if the sail might suffer a little. It really was a very exasperating time for him, I think. For instance, when we were first starting, while he busily sewed on one corner of the sail, Jakey and I, rather than admit we could not force the needles through the heavy cloth with our bare hands, tried to hammer through the tough material with rocks. There was a rather noisy scene when he later asked to borrow the needles we were using. Of course, it was all Papa's fault that we broke the needles, for he had not given us seaming palms.

"Don't you know that these damn things are hard to get?

From now on you keep your hands a mile away from those needles!"

"Yes, Papa."

"It's your fault," Jakey giggled as we walked down to the beach, for in a way it was funny and Papa had not spanked us.

"It isn't, either," I answered. "You broke the most needles!"

Jakey turned to me then and burst out laughing. I joined him and took his hand, and we ran to the lagoon, stripped off our clothes, and jumped into the cool water, splashing noisily while the fish fled in panic.

We were brought back to reality by Papa's sharp whistle. "Oh! Jakey, he's going to scold us again."

We walked to the house and stood in the doorway, *kakau* (clothes) in hands and water dripping down our brown naked bodies.

"Who told you to leave?" Papa asked without even looking up at us.

"We thought you didn't want us to help you any more."

"Hold those two ends." He pointed. "But first dry your hands."

What a fussy man, I thought, as if this piece of rag won't soon be wet. I looked at Jakey: his face was suppressing a smile.

We worked on *Panikiniki's* tremendous sail for two weeks, or rather *we* played with it while Papa worked on it. But since we served his food while he worked, and gave up sleeping together in the sitting room because the unfinished sail was left spread there every night, we took it for granted we had taken an active part in the making of one of the biggest sails in the South Seas.

During this time the Puka-Pukans wondered what Papa was up to, for although he usually unfolded his plans to his friends this time he meant to surprise them. He kept close to

his work, seldom venturing out of the house, sending the
children on errands if he needed anything.

"Maybe sick," the villagers murmured. We played our part
in the subterfuge by telling them Papa was busy writing a new
book about them but for them not to worry for soon he would
be able to join them in their card games and fishing.

Finally the big day arrived and, after running excitedly
through the village, telling everyone to come to our house
right away, we kids ran back to help Papa carry the sail into
the daylight. A curious crowd of thirty or forty people had
assembled outside our door, jabbering and speculating on the
mystery. Then Papa emerged carrying the front end of the
sail, his face sober for just a moment before breaking into an
uncontrolled grin. The people pressed around us, laughing
and making jokes about Papa's long exile while he was working
on the canvas.

Forty hands helped us carry *Panikiniki's* crowning glory
to the beach. Ropes were measured; one went from the boom to
Papa's seat in the stern, two others were stretched from the top
of the mast to the outrigger booms, another to the opposite side
of the foremost outrigger boom, and still another to the bow.

Apparently, Papa's secret had not been too well kept, for
Uncle Aumatangi was there with a beautiful carved wooden
bailer he had made for Papa in case the canoe took on water,
listing under the pull of the sail in a storm. It could also be
used when it rained. (The Puka-Pukans are the only people
who use wooden bailers. The other islanders use bully beef
cans and coconut shells.) The Puka-Pukans also had made for
us wooden paddles out of strong *tou* wood, paddles that were
very similiar to the ones warriors used when they traveled
from island to island centuries ago.

With cheering and applause the canoe was hauled into the
water. Then the mast was stepped in the bow, the paddles that

were lashed to the outrigger boom were untied, and the ropes coiled as if the canoe were a large schooner. Papa then told each of us children where we would always sit. That way we would not quarrel. Before we knew it we were pushed off, with the land falling quickly behind.

Nga sat directly in the rear, in front of Captain Frisbie, with nothing to do except help Elaine bail. Elaine had her little seat in dead center, across the hollowed hull of *Panikiniki*. Jakey sat in front of the mast, leaning on it, where he could keep a lookout for dangerous sharp coral heads. Since I was the heaviest I was given the honor of sitting on the outrigger boom, to help keep it down when the strong winds filled the sail and lifted the outrigger out of the water and up into the air. At such times Papa allowed the beam to stay up in the air half a minute or so while the other children listened to my excited screams. Later, on calm days, I sat alone, but when the northeasterly wind blew in gusts Jakey joined me. When it blew even stronger, I was forced to sit on the outrigger itself, my back resting on the wooden thongs that held the outrigger and the boom together. Jakey would then take my usual place on the boom. Sometimes we held hands to keep steady, and felt the wind wipe the salt water from our arms. Sitting there, we pretended we were flying high above the sea in an airplane, flying and bounding up and down in the midst of air sacs. We called it our Puka-Pukan seaplane, although we had just the vaguest idea of what an airplane really was.

And often we looked back at Papa with the mainsheet in his hand, its end under one foot, Nga crouched between his legs, enjoying life and not knowing exactly why. Elaine, with one elbow resting on the rim of the canoe while the other dragged in the water, sang happily to everybody.

The Puka-Pukans asked us why Papa sometimes tied the mainsheet around his body. They used to ask whether or not it hurt when he slackened the sail and the rope tightened around his back. We did not know the answer either, but Papa looked very heroic.

Noticing our stares of admiration, Papa smiled and spit tobacco juice, which made us a little sick to the stomach. We just could not understand how he could chew the stuff, but it gave him the air of an old mariner.

We spent many days working on *Panikiniki*. We gave our complete attention to her, scrubbing her after each sailing, covering her with coconut fronds and *ngayu* branches to keep the sun from burning the sennits and cracking her precious hull. And after each sailing we carefully took down the mast and carried it to its special corner in our sleeping house, where we could admire it and wait eagerly for the next time the wind would blow favorably.

Perhaps it was *Panikiniki* which gave Papa the inspiration to write *Song of the Wind*. Like many authors of prose, he enjoyed experimenting with verse. Of the many poems he wrote, this one comes closest to expressing the artistic feeling of the Papa we knew.

> *A ship at sea, a sailing craft well manned,*
> *With tanned and hardened men from southern climes,*
> *Sailed lightly through the calm untroubled sea;*
> *While softly blew the southern wind, and flapped*
> *The sails, and brushed the seamen's hardened cheeks.*
>
> *I stood upon the prow and gazed into*
> *The sea, and watched the listless billows break*
> *And foam and break again upon the ship.*
> *And as I watched the sun went down, and the stars*
> *And moon came out, and the wind of the sea*
> *Hummed softly to me, and I knew my love*

Had come; My Goddess of the Wind had come.
And so I lay upon the deck and gazed
Into the sea, and in the billows saw
My inspiration playing on the foam.
I gazed, and gazing loved, loving gazed,
And stretched mine arms to steal her from the wind.

The night was black, the ripples grew to waves
And broke, and crashed, and pounded on the ship.
I woke and heard the wild wind ripping through
The sails, and heard the seamen shout, and heard
The mast swing, creaking, groaning to and fro.
And then remembered I of how I stretched
My arms forth to the Goddess of the Wind:
Mayhap the wind revengeth for her own.

The gale increased with maddened violence,
And tossed our ship about as if it were
A chip of drift wood on the sea. I bound
Myself securely to the naked mast,
And placed my fate into my loved one's hands.
Then came a mighty blast and burst the ship,
And flung it in the sea. I felt her snow
White arms and silken hair, and then, but for
A second, saw her face, and knew no more.

The dawn, the crystal cloud-lit dawn, when all
Alone I drifted on the silent sea,
Fast bound upon the mast, and dazed and stunned.
The dawn—I woke and felt the sea breeze soft
Caress, and saw the stars blink lazily
And one by one go out before the sun.
Then from the east my inspiration came;
She rode within a chariot of gold,

Drawn by four dappled steeds, high spirited.
I looked and saw her silken tresses, saw
Her laughing eyes; and then she passed, and looked
Upon me once, and laughed, and drove away.

The sun arose in splendid glory; but
I closed mine eyes, and knew nor cared no more.

CHAPTER 15

A Game of Marbles

My large family is fat and happy. What a vast amount of tinned milk [my] children can drink in a day! They are getting rather expensive. But I don't care. I love the little brats. My youngest daughter . . . is learning to talk. Sometimes she gets sore as a boiled owl over some rank injustice, such as a complete insufficiency of jam on her bread, and toddling up to me, her fists clenched, her eyes flashing, she gives voice to her rage in an exasperated "blub-ul-ub-ul-ub!" I don't know how you felt about Charles and Robert when they were young and docile but I know that my . . . children are a never-ending source of pleasure.

(Papa's letter to his mother; Puka-Puka.)

Papa had a very clever way of calling us. Wherever we might be, on the beaches of the island building little houses, swimming outside the reef, or surfing, we could always hear that familiar undulating whistle. Others have tried unsuccessfully to imitate his whistle, but none could develop such a piercing sound. Whenever we heard Papa's whistle we would leave a game of marbles, or perhaps the task of gathering coconuts to be stored in the shed, to immediately run to him, flapping our arms and jumping over piles of dried coconuts.

One day, however, we disobeyed him. This time, we were deeply engrossed in a game of marbles in a coconut grove near our home. Papa strongly objected to our playing marbles because our fingernails became chipped and would look like dried fish scales, while our knees became grimy with black dirt. Still, we just could not leave when he whistled that day: it was so important that Nga and I win back our priceless tamanu-seed marbles, which we had gathered and treasured. (The dried tamanu seed makes a good substitute in Puka-Puka for the rare and expensive glass marble.)

Papa was standing in the doorway of the cookhouse, his hands resting on his bare hips, a little above his *maro*. He whistled for us to come, but I waved a hand to make him understand that this was very important, and please wait! We heard the whistle again, and this time it sounded sharper. Jakey, right after he shot Nga's king-size marble so hard it cracked, waved as I did, but still kept his eyes on the marbles. We were on our knees, surrounding the circle of marbles, each intently studying them, as if afraid they would pop right out of the circle and disappear.

Suddenly we heard not the whistle but an unpleasant yell: "Didn't you hear me?"

"Yes, Papa." Simultaneously we jumped and answered.

"Come here! Now."

Hurriedly we gathered our precious marbles into our dresses, Jakey stuffing his into his pants pockets. Then, as fast as our tough little bare feet would allow, we ran toward the bathhouse, hoping to avoid Papa as we knew quite well what was in store for us. But he called us and we had to go to him.

Papa pulled down our pants one by one and walloped us

hard, as if he were pounding the dust from a canvas sail. Our backsides hurt, making us see angry waves and hear howling winds. Our brown bottoms were now lobster red.

"Don't you know it's getting dark and you should be in the house by now?" Papa roared, awkwardly chasing us to the bathhouse, probably laughing at us as we rubbed our throbbing backsides. "The next time you are all so deaf I shall burn your marbles in the cookstove to brew my tea!"

He then walked to the open cookhouse and started supper. Through the cracks of the coconut-frond shutters we watched him and happily discovered that he was not burning our marbles and that he seemed back to normal again. We did not rejoice though, for our *kanos-kanos* were still sore.

"I told you, but you wouldn't listen! It was all your fault that Papa got angry and spanked us," I grumbled.

Elaine answered me resentfully; Nga attempted to hit Jakey just so they could be in the fight.

"Jakey told you, but you wouldn't listen," Elaine said, making a face. "You're always getting us in trouble!"

"Look"—I thrust my face in front of her—"you heard Papa whistle. If you were smart you wouldn't stay on hoping to win, then blame me for the spanking you got. *Tiemia* [Damn it]!"

"*Tiemia* yourself," Elaine retorted, roughly pushing me away.

"I'm going to tell Papa you said a bad word," Nga said to her quietly and innocently.

"Yeah, what about Johnny? She said it first."

"I don't care; *you* said it, too."

"Just because Johnny is bigger than me, that's why you're on her side, heh?" Elaine shouted at Nga, the most hateful person at the moment because she was so calm.

"I'm going to tell on you to Papa, you wait," Nga continued teasing, walking out the narrow doorway of the bathroom.

"You stop it! Johnny said it first!" Elaine screamed, tears beginning to blind her eyes.

"Stop that fight right now!" we heard Papa yell from the cookhouse. "And don't let me hear you kids swear and fight like wild pigs. Also, *don't* forget to hang your towels."

The towels were kept on the open top of the bathhouse so we would not run wet and naked to the sleeping house, shocking some of the religious missionaries living near us. After drying ourselves we ran bare-bottomed to wrap the colorful *pareus* around our waists, then emerged like a row of ducks and marched angelically toward the cookhouse.

We waited for Papa to say something first, noiselessly sipping our cups of weak New Zealand tea. When he finally mentioned that we needed more firewood, we immediately knew he was no longer angry, and we all began to laugh about the game of marbles.

CHAPTER 16

Tili

*. . . the young unmarried were gathered. A plaintive heathen
strain sounded from a copse of bush; farther on some one was
drumming a weird rhythm on a coconut shell while a girl and
a boy danced before him. I could hear laughing cries from
out on the reef and see shadowy figures here and there.*

(THE BOOK OF PUKA-PUKA, page 82.)

Cousin Tili was the nosy type of girl. She wanted to know
everything, even what the local parson thought about at night
and what he did between sermons. She had many times involved us in trouble stemming from other people's love affairs.
Sometimes she was so naughty she had to stay in hiding for
days because Mama Tala threatened to beat her.

Cousin Tili loved to include me in her adventures, for I
was nine and very curious. One Sunday morning, for example,
we left our Bibles under the coconut trees to hunt for jewelry
in the bushes.

Costume jewelry is rare on Puka-Puka. A Puka-Pukan
woman wears her limited jewelry on only a few important

occasions, such as a wedding or when she meets her lover in the
taeyinu bushes.

When two lovers secretly meet at night on the outer beaches,
or in the coconut groves, it is very important for them not
to be seen together. A love affair on Puka-Puka is so secret
that often no one suspects it for months, or even years. This
is very difficult on an island only a square mile in size.

Two lovers never look at each other in the daytime when
other people are around. One might assume that they are
ashamed of the love affair, but they aren't at all. People are
never ashamed of love in the South Seas. Their furtiveness
comes from their desire to own and share a secret, for secrets
are precious few on the small islands.

"Tiane," Tili confided as we walked away from Yato Village,
"I think my sister Vaevae has a sweetheart she meets at night."

"How do you know?"

"This morning she looked around for one of her earrings to
wear to church, acting as if it were lost in the house. But I
know. Do you want to find it with me? I think I know approximately where it is."

We searched the bushes, particularly under the young
coconut trees, for the overhanging fronds make a cozy lean-to.
We looked, too, for split fronds laid together so that the mid-
ribs are on the outside and the long, crackly leaves crisscrossed
on the inside. This makes a most comfortable mattress.

Soon we found a likely spot, and among the leaves we found
a single hairpin, which is just as valuable to a Puka-Pukan
woman as a diamond.

"We'll keep this and wait for the word that So-and-So has
lost one," Tili whispered excitedly.

We continued our search. We found many split fronds, discovered a cheap chipped pearl necklace at one cozy meeting
place, and finally Vaevae's earring at another.

Rushing home, we asked Papa who had bought a pearl necklace from the trading station. He told us it was the parson's daughter, who was engaged to a Rarotongan boy. Then we went to Tili's home and showed Vaevae her lost earring. As we expected, she ran after us, screaming at the top of her lungs that it was not our business to go snooping around. We let her chase us through Yato Village, in and out of people's open cookhouses, dodging coconut trees and wandering chickens that flew under our feet.

"Stop! Stop!" Vaevae howled for all the neighborhood to hear. "If you let a word of this out, I'll kill both of you!"

"But what were you doing in the bushes last night? Who was you with?" Tili asked, laughing and ducking behind a tree.

Of course, Vaevae finally had to tell us in order to get her earring back, but we kept her secret.

Some time later Cousin Tili announced, "Tiane, we're planning to sneak over to Motu Kotawa the next full-moon night. Can you get away?"

This was the best plan she had ever concocted, and the most exciting. The most mischievous, too, since it was not the season to visit Motu Kotawa. The island was *tapu* except during the time of the coconut-gathering festival, and I was not supposed to even think of sneaking away to spend a night on an islet; especially without my guardian, Jakey.

Two nights before the full moon Tili, two of her girl friends, and I and three husky but harmless boys met on the beach at Yato to discuss plans. When the meeting was over, we knew what to do. The boys were to find a suitable canoe. The paddles we would borrow from Tili's father—without his knowing it, of course. I was chosen to do the fast talking when we approached the caretaker on Motu Kotawa. My creativeness in telling lies was finally being put to an important test. We would leave from

Yato Beach at four o'clock on the afternoon of the full moon. No one would think much of our sailing away because every day children went out into the lagoon to dive for mantrap clams or to sit on the corals in the middle of the lagoon.

Two days later, on that afternoon in April of 1941, the great expedition began. To get away from the house I pretended to walk nonchalantly to the w.c., but my nosy brother sensed the excitement in the seaweed-scented air and followed me.

I playfully ran away, hoping to dodge around the houses and trees, then slip away in the waiting canoe. But Jakey kept right behind me.

"I know what you're doing. You're going to run away and have fun without me. Take me or I'll tell Papa 'bout the night you rubbed noses with my friend Peni."

Time was passing fast. The others must be waiting impatiently. I ran toward Yato Beach, with Jakey trailing behind, saying, "Just tell me where you're going."

By this time we were at the beach, and instead of answering him I looked at my companions and then back at Jakey and said, "Okay—come on!" And we all jumped into the canoe and pushed off into the deep water of the lagoon.

We approached Motu Kotawa just as the sun was dipping into the rolling waves, Jakey having done most of the paddling for the four or five miles, in appreciation of our kindness in allowing him to join us. We reached the strip of bare bleached sand, and as we spilled out to lift the canoe ashore a thundering voice came from somewhere in the darkening trees.

"And where do you think you're going?"

We dropped the canoe and ran to hide behind the bushes.

"Do I have to beat you to remind your empty coconut heads that this is *not* the season for visiting?" After a few moments the same voice was heard again: "Who in the name of the good God sent you here? Okay. Come out of there and speak up!"

He sounded terribly mean. I thought, though, that I might pacify him by the mention of a few twists of tobacco and a couple of sticks of matches.

Tili, with her teeth clattering, nudged me and pushed me out from behind the bushes that protected us. Then I heard her pray to God to soften the caretaker's heart.

Stepping from behind the bushes, I looked around and still saw no one. I took four steps forward and yelled at the top of my voice, "We are playing hide-and-go-seek." There was no answer. I felt foolish at having spoken to someone I could not see, and I wasn't even certain there was a real man there. I looked back. Tili and Jakey were staring at me with wide eyes in the gathering gloom. I called again.

"Please let us hide here overnight. We promise not to steal any fruit from the plantation. [The plantation consisted of two lime trees, about twelve papaya trees, and quite a few frangipani trees.] And we'll sleep in the *are ropa* [the young people's house], the boys and the girls surely separated." Still no answer. "It's too late to go back anyway."

I began to doubt that he was still there in the trees. Gaining courage, I yelled, "Will you let us stay then? I'll get you some twisted tobacco and matchsticks from Papa."

An awful-looking man climbed down from a young, short coconut tree. He had been sitting on the top of the tree, watching every movement we had made from the time we were halfway across the lagoon.

"Okay. But I am still the boss around here. I'll give you permission to catch a few birds, coconut crabs, and enough *utos* for dinner."

The children burst from behind the bushes, laughing and jumping up and down like *matikus* (small but very active birds that hop about on the beaches of Puka-Puka).

That night was both wild and restrained. Wild because we

were there without permission of our parents and restrained because we were trying our best to be ladies and gentlemen in front of the caretaker. Jakey and I postponed thinking about what Papa would do until the next day.

At about seven o'clock we found ourselves in the midst of a *Puka* (hernandia) grove. It was not dark, for the moon smiled upon us. The *Puka* trees were very big, and seemed to reach the sky, and birds crowded the delicate branches. The crickets were busy at their sharp calls while thousands of birds were in deep sleep, with a few here and there squawking, as if to say, "Hey there, don't bother this branch; it's mine. Can't you see?"

We were particularly hungry for *tapukus*—the young birds that are so tender and fat. The four boys climbed the smooth trees and were soon lost to view. There was no noise after they had reached the sanctuary, for they were trying to avoid the twigs or dried leaves caught on the branches. Then the dead birds came falling through the leaves, warning us who were below to run for shelter next to a tree trunk. Afterward in the semi-darkness we felt among the dead leaves for the feathery bundles.

Soon we had made a big fire on the outer beach, where the people of Walé could not see it. We roasted the birds over the hot coals by inserting a barkless stick about four inches long through the bird's mouth. The fat dripped on the hot fire—and the delicious odor started our mouths watering. As the birds cooked, we wiped off the tasty fat with *utos* and ate it.

Such a feast!

As we ate and thought up ways of stealing papayas and limes to take home to Papa we saw at some distance, silhouetted in the moonlight, a mother turtle crawling heavily out of the sea to a cluster of trees, to lay her one hundred eggs.

Mama turtle must have weighed close to five hundred pounds, for in her struggle to climb the slight rise of the beach she puffed and hissed. We decided not to capture her, but planned to take some of her delicious fishy eggs.

We slept in the *are ropa,* a house built on stilts, partitioned so that boys could sleep on one half of the second floor and the girls on the other half. To make sure that no foolishness went on, there was a wide gap between the two halves. But we managed to swing like monkeys on the crossbeams, so that we could all sleep together. I could not join the love games because Jakey was by my side. Besides, I was several years younger than the others.

And early the next morning, after we had wrapped papayas and limes in *kotawa* (bird's-nest plant) leaves, we filled a small basket with turtle eggs to take home to our relatives, certain that no one else on Walé would know about it.

Before we sailed back to Walé, our friend the caretaker carefully inspected our canoe and, finding nothing for which to reprimand us, shoved us into the deep water. And when he had turned away, we took from under our dresses and hats the papayas, limes, and little packages of turtle eggs. Did he not wonder why we had sat so still in the canoe as he inspected?

And, fortunately, Papa was not the least bit angry or disappointed in Jakey and me. He was particularly proud that we had fooled the caretaker on Motu Kotawa and brought back such delicacies. I decided to wait until later before telling him he owed the caretaker tobacco and matches.

CHAPTER 17

Grandmother Tala

We live such sensual lives in the South Seas, with Nature showering her blessings on us, that we forget the grim chances of life: we forget that there can be hunger, and pain, and death, until, all at once, it is brought home to us, appallingly, that these things exist.

(MY TAHITI, page 268.)

When my great-grandmother Tangi died in Roto, her daughter, Mama Tala, and the family in Yato planned to go to Roto for an overnight stay. Papa gave permission for me to go with Tala. I was surprised at his generosity, since it meant associating with people who were strong in their fear of ghosts and Papa did not want us to be afraid of ghosts.

Walking to Roto, Mama Tala told us that she had known of Tangi's death before she received the news. The previous night in her dream she had seen vague, silent people in long black gowns carrying a coffin, but she could not see their faces. When she ran to them and asked whom they carried, a voice answered from within the coffin, "No, please, child.

I mustn't even pause to say good-by." At that, Mama Tala had awakened to await the bearer of bad news. If she had dreamed the same dream of a younger person who was *not* ill she could have broken the death spell, according to legend, by cutting the young hair on the back of her own neck. So Mama Tala believed, and who was to deny it?

Reaching Roto, we could hear the wailing and the chanting of the women and old men. Custom demanded the younger men sit quietly out of the way after they kissed the deceased. Young children sat idle and bored, restricted from play since they had to pay homage to Great-grandmother Tangi. Everyone spoke softly and whispered his words, careful not to say anything to offend the dead.

Mama Tala entered the house where the newly arrived mourners were gathering, awaiting their turn to visit the deceased. There she was given the details of her mother's death. Then she walked toward her mother, kissed both her closed eyes, dropped to the floor, and crawled backward on her knees a couple of steps, lifted her arms, bent her waist so that the tips of her fingers touched the new pandanus mat, and began chanting. Tears came to her eyes, and the rhythmic chant turned into a confusion of words: "You have born and now you have left me. Will you in your long sleep guard the family left behind!"

She chanted from morning through the afternoon and late into the night, weeping steadily and yet fairly well composed. She also stopped for an occasional rest, to chat quietly with the others who sat around the deceased, fans in hands to chase the flies. When she was conversing, it seemed hard to believe that she grieved the loss of her mother, but then, all of a sudden, in the middle of a sentence she would throw her arms into the air and begin repeating the rhythmic motions and the chant.

By early morning the following day my great-grandmother was ready for burial. She was carried in an unpolished, home-made coffin, fashioned from the trunk of a hernandia tree, to the burial ground, with a line of people following. The coffin was placed in a deep hole, the parson prayed and threw sand onto the coffin, and everybody else did likewise.

We returned to Tangi's home to receive our share of the food bought with the money donated by sympathetic friends. That night, people gathered to sing mournful hymns as the climax to the funeral.

Back in Tala's house in Yato, Mama Tala asked me to join her in the cookhouse as she prepared a simple lunch of boiled pork and taro. This sounds tasteless, but after one has mashed it well in fermented coconut cream it is a food fit for the chiefs.

"Last night, Angavale (a more affectionate way of addressing a grandchild than Makopuna), I dreamed of your mother. It seems that she is happy with the way your papa is taking care of you children but that she would rather he marry again. I told her that I'd relay the message but she said, no, let him decide for himself."

I cuddled close to Mama Tala and felt a longing for our mother. I began to cry, as I usually did in those days whenever I was reminded of Mama, which was often, since Papa frequently talked to us about her.

"Mama Tala! Mama Tala!" I cried. "I want to give Mama

some flowers for her hair. Will you please help me pick flowers for her?"

We walked back to Roto Village by way of the inner road and into the taro patches, where grew the beautiful white *tiare Maoris* (gardenias). As we plucked the scented blossoms, I made a short *yei* for Mama's head. I wrapped it in a taro leaf and tied it with a string from the midrib of a fallen coconut frond. We walked to Ngake and the graveyard. My feet trembled with fear as we unavoidably walked over gravel-covered graves and dodged the coral slabs that were the headstones. Mama Tala had no fear, for Puka-Pukans have no fear of the dead as long as it is daylight. But they greatly fear the dead spirits at night, and what Tala and I were doing would *never* be done after the sun had set.

We arrived at Mama's simple grave, peaceful in the early afternoon. In those days I believed that the dead could hear us, and would answer us in our dreams. I kissed Mama's grave and then set the *yei* on her headstone, placing a single *tiare* at the foot of the stone with the thought I knew she heard: This is to put on your ear, Mama, when you visit Papa in your dream. I kissed the white grave again, the white pebbles brought from the clean seashore, then bid her good-by.

Mama Tala carried me home, for I was still sobbing, and explained everything to Papa.

"From now on, Johnny," he said, "it is best you stay away from seeing dead people. It reminds you too much of dear Mama; it makes you too unhappy. Mama wants you to be happy always."

He gently scratched my head until I fell asleep.

CHAPTER 18

War on Lice

*When Nga died I told my friends that I proposed to keep my
children and bring them up without a woman's help. If my
wife could bathe my son I opined that I could bathe my
daughters, but as all my children could bathe themsleves it
should be necessary for me only to see that they did so. In
other things I proposed to teach my children to take care of
themselves. My friends were skeptical. They believed I would
soon be fed up and would remarry or hire a nursemaid. Hire
a nursemaid! For myself, perhaps, but certainly not for my
children; and I need no nursemaid to take care of me so long
as I have the children for the job.*

(THE ISLAND OF DESIRE, page 175.)

Even though Papa sometimes slapped our faces until we
could hear the ringing of distant bells and smacked our backsides until the tough skin looked like red leather, he was still
the kindest of fathers. I must admit the spanking hurt very
little. But I bet his hands stung, for our brown bottoms were,
like most Puka-Pukan behinds, tough as sharkskin.

We could have run away from him, as most Puka-Pukan
kids do when facing discipline, but we did not want to make
Papa run that hard or climb trees, as many of the mothers
and fathers were often required to do to carry out punishments.
Puka-Pukan parents rarely let their children get the upper
hand. Besides, Papa would have had little success in climbing
a tree; he would have looked like a lanky young tern trying
to get back into its nest. He would have had no trouble
swimming after us, but climbing a tree was strictly out of the
question and our pride in him would not let us subject him to
such an experience.

Our cousin Tili, however, obviously did not feel this same
concern for her parents. She was very independent, and was
Papa's favorite Puka-Pukan relative, being his sister-in-law
even though only thirteen. One day Tili just did not feel like
picking the black lice from Mama Tala's gray hair, and ran
away from her after telling Tala that all the fingers on the
island could not clean her hair! Soon the village was amused
to see fat Mama Tala, huffing and wheezing, waddling after
Tili, in and out of people's shacks. Finally Tili, tiring of
leading Mama Tala in this unequal race, climbed up a
coconut tree, giggling at her mother's consternation.

"You come down right this minute or I'll send your brother
after you!" Mama Tala screamed for everyone in the village
to hear. All the while, she kept puffing the way the pigs in
our sty did when they fought over some choice bit of coconut
meat. Then she tried throwing stones at Tili, without success.

"If I were not so fat and old," she admitted without shame,
hands on her round hips and legs far apart, "you'd get it, young
lady. Wait till you come down. You can't stay up there forever
and ever. God help me, you can't! And don't think you're
going to eat in my house tonight. *Aue, koe! Ea ra koe e aka
pena ai?*" ("Oh, you! Why do you ever act this way?")

Five minutes or so later she wandered off to another house and found somebody else's daughter to pick the ugly, crawling, greasy black lice, saying, "Now why can't my own daughter do this? I brought her into this world, cooked her food, washed her clothes, and someday will marry her off, and after that I shall probably take care of her brats." Then she scratched her head. "Over here, Vaetianiu [Thin Legs]. I can feel the scoundrel crawling! Aha! Let me have the overfed pig." Taking the louse and glaring at it as if it were man's worst enemy, she placed it upon her flat tongue and expertly slid the bug down between her front teeth, where she bit it so hard the clicking together of her teeth could be heard.

How Papa hated that! He warned us once that if he ever saw *his* children biting lice he would brush their teeth with castor oil and soap. That was enough to scare us.

During our monthly hair wash with kerosene, which temporarily rid our hair of the tenacious little bugs, Papa used to swear that we were never, never to play with the Puka-Pukans again.

"Don't let me see you kids play with those lice breeders any more, understand?" he howled, and plunged our heads, plunk, into the kerosene can.

"Look at that filthy mess!" he cried, pointing at the lice that were frantically drowning in the kerosene, and for which we felt sorry. "Do you like the look of that?"

"Yes! Oh no, Papa!" we blubbered.

"Why are you crying?" he asked, scratching our heads to find the lice still hidden there.

"I have kerosene in my eyes."

"Then close them!"

"Yes, Papa."

How he hated hair infested with lice. And how we hated to have our hair washed with the pungent kerosene. After the poor lice had all been killed, our heads would actually feel light, and we would no longer have to avoid scratching them. For often when Papa happened to be around we would try not to scratch our heads for fear he would notice it and decide it was time to give us another kerosene wash. We preferred to let Mama Tala feast on them.

One night after a kerosene hair shampoo, Jakey, Elaine, some neighborhood kids, and I walked down to the beach to play hide-and-go-seek, sing songs, and finally swim in the rippleless lagoon. Papa did not know we were out of the house, for we rarely left at night without permission. He thought, or so we believed, that we were fast asleep under the mosquito net. I still remember the way he called us when he discovered only Nga asleep under the gigantic net.

"Johnny! Jakey! Elaine!" we heard him bellow from the door of our sleeping house.

"Yes, Papa." Three frightened voices came out of the darkness.

"Come here! Now!"

"Yes, Papa," three guilty voices replied.

We saw his trembling body half wrapped in a *pareu,* standing in the doorway, red with anger. He pulled off our *pareus* one by one and spanked us, five steady, consecutive slaps. We marched into the storage room, hands rubbing our bottoms. We had not been spanked this way in a long time!

After a while the bamboo door slowly opened. Potiki Nga walked in and sat among us, her sleepy face showing her disgust with the whole business. She had been awakened by the shouting and become lonely under our big mosquito net. Sitting in the semi-dark room, idly picking up bits of gravel with my toes, I could hear the young people singing outside and splashing the water as they swam. Later it grew quiet as they scattered among the *ngayu* trees, to whisper, to love, and very likely to fall asleep in the bushes, noses together, believing it was what the older people did.

"Who told you to go out there after dark?" Papa suddenly shouted through the wall, causing a small earthquake in the room.

No one spoke.

"Well, aren't you going to answer me?"

Reluctantly Jakey whispered, barely audibly, "Johnny did, Papa." He looked at me, asking for forgiveness.

"Johnny, you stay in there. The rest of you may come out now."

One by one they walked to the door as I watched. I felt I might never see them again, so I decided the only thing to do was to walk across to Motu Kotawa and commit suicide by jumping over the reef at the most dangerous part and join Mama in her happy world. I said a short prayer to Mama to help me. The other three looked at me from the doorway as if they, too, thought it would be the last they would ever see of me.

Later, through a crack in the pandanus wall, I watched Papa sitting on his bunk, leaning back against two kapok pillows. His chin, the pointed and distinguished chin, was on his right knee, his eyes toward my prison. He sat motionless for a few minutes, lost in thought. Suddenly he buried his head in his hands, digging the fingernails into his hair. Perhaps his thoughts then were similar to those when he wrote James Norman Hall: "I am afraid she might turn into a good-for-nothing whore if she stays here too long." And to Uncle Charles: "I hope she will keep her stinking virginity for another three years."

He was afraid lest I might, at an early age, fall in love, marry, start raising grandchildren for him, and spend the rest of my life chained to Puka-Puka, without a chance of seeing the rest of the world. Once, later, he even said to me, "Johnny, wait until you're nineteen or twenty before you play around. Wait until you're in a more civilized country. The boys here are so full of diseases. You know that, for you've helped me cure many cases of syphilis. Set a good example for your younger sisters."

I continued looking through the pandanus wall. Elaine, Jakey, and Nga were seated directly in front of me, so that I could smell the coconut oil from their bodies. Occasionally Jakey would scratch the wall with his little finger and I would answer him by scraping the flat pandanus sticks, not knowing exactly why, since I should have been angry with him. Papa looked thoughtfully at the other children, his lips slightly parted by a smile. Then he motioned with his hand for Jakey to tell me that my prison sentence had been suspended.

Jakey hurried into my little cell as Papa's forgiving voice called, "You may come out now."

I did not answer or show any sign of gladness.

"Papa said for you to come out!" Jakey repeated excitedly.

"I don't want to," I answered sharply.

"Please, Tiane, come out. Don't let him spank you again."

"I don't care. He can spank me all he wants." By this time Jakey was crying. He put his hands around my waist, lifting my stubborn body, half carrying, half dragging me.

"Come, Johnny. I'll sleep by you tonight, and tomorrow you can go sailing with Potika and me; you won't be in the way, I promise you."

I became selfish. I wanted Jakey to make more promises, to continue pleading. But finally I gave in to his wishes.

Walking out the door of the storage room, I could see from the corner of my eye that Papa had already forgiven me. At first I walked slowly, but suddenly I ran to his outstretched arms, feeling very foolish but completely happy.

CHAPTER 19

Copra Making

All the settlements were deserted, and while I was break-
fasting Benny came to me to explain that he could not work
in the store during the coming month because it was the law
of the island that every man, woman, and child must go to
their islets, or, as was the case with Central Village, go to their
temporary village on the sea side of Puka-Puka.

(THE BOOK OF PUKA-PUKA, page 69.)

During the middle of the hurricane season, from November
through March, when no schooners visited the island, the
people of all three villages of Puka-Puka enthusiastically
began what amounted to a copra festival.

On the appointed day, usually shortly after New Year's,
they sailed across the lagoon to Motu Kotawa and Motu Ko,
where the people had divided the islands into communal plots
belonging to this or that village. The men and women sailed
their outrigger canoes—filled to the rims with clothing, empty
copra sacks, knives, and cooking utensils—across the great
four-mile inland lake while the children walked the reef at

low tide, gathering periwinkles and spearing fish trapped in the tide pools.

Months had passed since these two *motus* with their temporary villages had been occupied. A feeling, when first entering the village, of discovering something ancient and mysterious filled us with delightful chills. I still had not forgotten how frightened we had been the night we spent alone in the deserted village, with only the caretaker as company.

The shutters of all the sleeping houses were down, the houses had accumulated cobwebs on the ceilings and molds on the posts. Chickens had turned wild, and ran into hiding at our approach. Birds who had made nests on the nearby trees now had to bear the noise of civilization again, and risk their lives and those of their young ones. But in no time the shutters were pulled up and the wind in excitement rushed through the open windows as it once again invaded the musty homes. Fires were lit in the cookhouses, and the rats scrambled in confusion into the dark corners or ran outside to climb the coconut trees.

The first and most important preparation for the copra festival was the rebuilding of old racks and the making of new racks for the drying of coconuts. Then, when this was done, the chiefs of the village ordered the coconut gathering to commence. Exuberant families ran from their houses to the coconut groves, yelling at the top of their voices and clapping their hands. Each family staked out a small section of the coconut trees. The competition was keen for, although the coconut trees belonged to the people, the gatherers were paid only for the amount of nuts they actually collected and turned into copra.

It was a wonderful sight to watch: bodies bending, hands speedily reaching for the dried nuts and hastily throwing them toward family piles. Sometimes all one could see was the nuts flying through the air. As long as one had lifted a coconut off the ground and thrown it toward the *putunga* (pile), no one else had the right to touch that coconut. But as long as there were untouched coconuts, anybody could fight for them, and there were many conflicts and long discussions over a single coconut. Also, it was a rule that no one was to climb the trees to shake or pull down any of the nuts, but there were always some people who cheated.

The coconuts were husked in no time by the men, who passed them to the women, who with quick swings of their heavy butcher knives cut the shells into perfect halves. Then they scooped out the spongy center and put the *utos* in separate clean baskets for eating. The shells were later carried to the beaches to soak a day or two in the sea, so that the meat would be tougher and less liable to rot during the drying process.

I remember diving into the clear sea, hunting for baby *utos* left in the coconut shells and liking the taste of the salted,

marble-size things. And sometimes we children took big bites of coconut meat, intentionally leaving tooth marks in the meat for the men to swear about later. Of course, the men would guard their piles of coconuts, so we delighted in swimming under water from a long distance away to pretend to steal the floating coconuts.

During the period that the coconuts were soaking, there was little for us children to do but re-explore the island or play *pio,* a game in which two teams line up and face each other. One team is in deep water, standing on a rock, while the other team is in shallow water, about twenty yards away. The members of the deep-water team dive from the rock and try to swim to the shallow water, where they can stand up, without being touched on the way by the opposing team. Some dive as deep as possible, in the hope that the defenders from the shore-side team will be unable to see them. Each one who gets past the opposing team without being caught scores a point. Ten points win a game.

Two days after being put in the lagoon the coconut shells were taken from the water and laid on the high wooden racks which had been erected on the beaches, where the sun was strongest. The meat faced the sun, and when rain threatened all hands helped turn the coconut shells upside down to prevent them from getting wet and thus losing some of the coconut meat's precious oiliness. At night they were automatically turned upside down.

It took several weeks for the coconuts to dry completely without losing their oil. Then the meat, curling inward, away from the shell, was spooned out with wooden spatulas, cut into small pieces, and stored in copra sacks. There is no reason to think that this ancient method of making copra has been improved upon today in Puka-Puka.

While nature was curing the coconut meat—the people

found time to enjoy the festival. Groups of them would practice the singing of hymns and play the American games Papa
had taught them, like baseball and poker. The children,
however, had to continue school, learning to read nursery
rhymes and to add four and six, often using dried coconuts
to illustrate the problem.

Just before the end of the gathering season Papa returned to
Walé to weigh the copra being shipped to the main island
from Motu Ko and Motu Kotawa. I remember that once he
became suspicious of the extreme weight of a copra sack and,
kicking it hard, hurt his toes on a rock at the bottom of it. His
fury was indescribable. The color of his face changed several
times, as the color of an octopus changes.

"Just for that I shall lower the price of copra!" he bellowed.

From then on he had all the copra sacks emptied on a mat
to discourage further cheating. Also, he worked out little
tricks of his own to keep the price of copra down to a fair level.

Papa had built a small radio that miraculously worked. One
day as he listened to the news of a disaster in Europe, the excited tone of the announcer attracted a small group of men,
who crowded around the radio although they were unable to
understand the words. Finally one blurted out in excitement,
"Ropati, Ropati! What is the man chanting so angrily about?"

"Too bad! Too bad!" Papa sadly shook his head. "He is
saying the price of copra has gone down again."

CHAPTER 20

Papa Speaks English

*After a few months on a coral atoll the world in general is just
as far distant as a planet, and is looked upon with much the
same attitude. News heard from other countries is but history,
to be summed up unemotionally; all people but the bizarre
little savages about me become as the remembrance "of a tale
heard faintly from dead lips"; the remembrance of my own past
is no more than that of a book I have read; and lastly my associ-
ates are no more than so many wild things. In such a situation
imagine then what introspective broodings one must get into,
what almost endless trains of thought must pass through one's
mind, and what startling revelations must come.*

(Puka-Puka: April 1925; Papa's letter to his brother.)

When the schooner *Tiare Taporo* arrived, Papa was once
again the talk of the villages. All the Puka-Pukans, from the
very young to those with wrinkles on their tanned faces, took up
comfortable positions in front of our thatched house on the

beach, waiting and watching for Papa's appearance. We waited, too, of course. When he finally emerged, it was with brief case in hand, and he was wearing white starched shorts and a T shirt, revealing his sunburned arms and legs. On his feet were brown sandals and on his head was a white polished helmet that made him look like an African hunter we once had seen in a magazine picture.

We were awe-struck when Papa walked toward the beach to be the first to greet the schooner mooring beyond the reef. He seemed to have become something of a stranger himself, to have separated a little from us and our world. We laughed to see Papa's tanned toes wiggling uncomfortably in the sandals, knowing that he was just waiting for the moment when he could take them off. We studied the creases of his stiff starched shirt, wishing it would stay pressed and not wrinkle in the hot sun, because we wanted him to look handsome. I felt sorry for the washerwoman though, suspecting that he was cursing her under his breath, for he had asked her again and again *not* to starch his shirts so that they felt like sailcloth.

Papa was like a great king, followed by submissive if curious subjects.

"Are they *your* kids?" I sometimes overheard newcomers say when they saw Papa pointing proudly to us. "They look very much like natives!"

"Yes, ma'am; you've never seen blacker and more beautiful natives." Then in Puka-Pukan he would call, "Hey there, Hardpan Jake, show how white and sharp your teeth are, but don't scare the *popaas!*"

The newcomers looked at us in surprise, with scarcely veiled smirks on their faces, and asked, "Where's their mother?" perhaps expecting to be shown an incredibly savage woman.

If Papa was angry with his pompous guests he did not show it. I can't imagine what the *popaas* thought as we followed them, fighting for a chance to walk in their footsteps on the dusty paths. It was considered a great game to walk on the white visitor's footsteps. Sometimes we became brave enough to walk backward in front of them, watching their grim faces and staring with some interest at their mouths, especially those of the women because they looked so unusually red. But we ran behind trees when they pointed to us, afraid that they meant harm.

The Puka-Pukans were amazed and proud of the way Papa spoke English with the newcomers. He seemed never to stop talking! He demanded news of the latest epidemic in the Cook Islands; he asked questions about the "outside," about who was declaring war on whom and who desired to rule the world this year.

Watching through the coconut-leaf shutters of our house, we wondered what he and his strange acquaintances were drinking in the little red bottles, for we had never seen beer in bottles, since the Puka-Pukans used scrubbed kerosene tins for brewing. Even then, when I could not speak English, I had memorized his famous words, "Come on, please, say something, anything. I'm afraid I've been doing all the talking." Then without waiting for an answer he continued to ask more questions, with no sign whatsoever of apology on his face.

And when the ship sailed away to another island, Papa turned, for English conversation, to old William, the only Puka-Pukan who spoke and understood a little of this language we thought so difficult and funny. He made up conversations, pretending that old William was a professor with a vocabulary of sixty thousand words. And if he did not understand Papa old

William would change the subject by asking in a nonchalant manner, "Gimme annuder beah, heh, Ropati-tané?" But Papa kept on with his philosophical conversation: "Listen: There is a light of the truth, the elusive truth, in each one of us, or rather seen by each one. Each one follows it apace, *dumbly, wordlessly,* and then an inexorable fate steps in and he must find a matrix for the abstract." Old William would nod his head.

"He formulates it in his own cloddy material contraptions, makes it into an image, a church, a word, a book, a dogma. Then, imbecile! He believes in his image because he once saw the light and beetle-headedly thought of his image at the same time. Here's the metaphor, William. Take a piece of glass and hold it before the lamp. The glass gives no light, but it is iridescent with the light of the lamp. Why, after the light is blown out, worship the glass? It is my serious opinion, given to you confidentially, that the world of men is a world of vapid, banal, imbecilic, effete asses!"

After this, old William would struggle to move his three hundred pounds of solid body, throw his bare arms upward, and loudly say, "Thar you go again, talking 'bout kelosene lamp."

Sometimes old William bragged to the neighbors of how well he could speak English. He used to mutter in English, and the neighbors ignored him completely, with a slight wave of the hand, saying, "Oh, you're just making up a language of your own." At that, old William indignantly pointed a finger at the sky and said, "If you believe what you say, why the hell don't you follow me to Ropati-tané's house and listen to the two of us talk?"

He was sensitive in his old age, for something seems to happen to Puka-Pukan men after they reach middle age.

It is not unusual to see a man complain childishly about the disappearance of a rusty old fishhook.

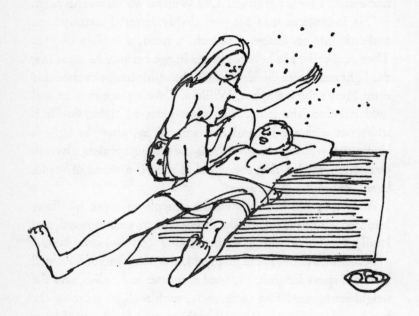

"Can't you do something about this? It is the only one I have, and now I can't go fishing."

Then, pouting, he will drag himself out of the house to the water's edge to sit on the white sand, digging his big toes into the sugary beach, muttering threats against the culprit who stole his fishhook, until the warm sun and lapping waves lull him to sleep.

If his wife wants this nonsense to stop within the week, she either runs from house to house, begging for another rusty hook, or she exuberantly spanks the handiest child, loudly accusing him of stealing the hook. This gives her husband satisfaction and he can then go back to carving new fishhooks from mother-of-pearl shells or weaving sennits from dried coconut husks. But most likely he will make himself comfortable under a shady, fruit-laden pandanus tree and go back to sleep.

It is quite common to see a Puka-Pukan man fall asleep with the sun still at its brightest while his wife quietly runs her hard-working hand through his black hair, swatting the flies as they insistently land on his wide-open mouth, undiscouraged by his thundering snore. I think Puka-Pukan men snore the loudest of any in the world.

Sometimes when old William exercised his vocal cords while asleep, the breakers pounding over the reef were reduced, by comparison, to the whispering of shy wavelets.

And when old William held a conversation, his face, as he spoke, was like a changing tapestry. His admiration of beautiful women and the twinkle in his eyes would indicate thoughts of romance. Then perhaps he would think of a night spent with Viivii, and he would remember that she married someone else. His face would darken and cloud over. "Bah, she doesn't understand life; she married another because she doesn't understand life!" Then his dark brown eyes would twinkle with the joyful

reminiscences of youthful days at sea, as if he could still feel
the excitement of harpooning a wandering whale. I could sit
for hours and watch old William talk and chant the soothing
Puka-Pukan's hymns.

CHAPTER 21

The Lagoon

The clamoring sea birds broke the thread of my musings.
I started to my feet; and as I gazed over the sea, contentment
gave place to a feeling of utter isolation. The stars had shifted
far to westward; only a pool of moonlight glowed above the
horizon.

(Papa's letter to his brother, dated February 1934.)

While we were living on Motu Kotawa, Papa would often
get up very early in the morning to sit on the beach at the edge
of the lagoon, leaving us four children still asleep on the living-
room floor. Sometimes, if one of us awakened early, we could
hear him talking and singing quietly to the fathomless sky.
Perhaps he hoped that in return he would be granted enthu-
siasm to write, for his work was going slowly.

One early morning, when the sun was not yet quite over the
dwarf *ngayu* bushes around our house, I got up and, putting on
a *pareu*, went out to the beach to join him. As I sat down in
the night-chilled sand, Papa put his arm around me and said,
"The sunrise is the most beautiful part of the day, Johnny.

Too bad it doesn't last longer. It inspires me to write beautiful things—but they evaporate with the sun's ascent."

He gazed at the red-tinged lagoon water and then added, "Or if I do write them, they seem commonplace by 10:00 A.M. What a great mystery is the dawn that allows us for a brief moment to catch the beauty that is in the everyday."

After a few more minutes he stood up slowly and, clapping his hands together, said, "Well, I won't be able to do any writing today with all these morbid thoughts, so how about a swim out to the middle of the lagoon?"

Jumping up before he had a chance to change his mind, I ran back to the house, yelling and whooping, while Papa came laughing right behind me, calling, "Come on, kids! Come on! Let's take a swim!"

Before Jakey, Elaine, and Nga were quite awake, we were eating a breakfast of husked green coconuts and ship's biscuits soaked in the sweet water of the nuts. It was a good breakfast, and one that would not slow us in the water.

Soon we were slipping into the lagoon, allowing our naked bodies to fully awaken at the cool touch of the sea. We swam steadily, in short strides, toward the bottom, and when the four of us were tired and breathless we would hold onto Papa's *maro*. Of course, when Papa decided to dive thirty feet down we were automatically pulled along, helping him kick and push the sea away so that we could reach the bottom and be up again in a matter of seconds. But when we ran out of breath, particularly Elaine and Nga, who were only six and four years old, we would tap Papa on the back and let go. This way he did not worry when he suddenly found us gone.

About a mile and a half out in the middle of the lagoon we stopped to dog-paddle and rest on some live coral heads that had grown, over many years, into mushroom shapes. Soon Papa was giving us lessons on how to swim free style, and also tried to teach us the crawl. Jakey learned speedily, but Elaine, Nga, and I gave up in despair. Little Nga, particularly, found the dog paddle much more practical for her needs. Papa also showed us different ways of diving off the coral. His hands were held together against his head or straight by his side, with feet tensed. He resembled a gangling frigate bird going head first into the sea. Then we showed him comical ways of jumping off, which came quite naturally to us since most Polynesian children are born clowns in the water.

After an hour or so of this we set about getting our morning snack. Taking Papa's pocketknife, which was carried in his *maro*, we dove to the bottom to unhinge *pauas* (mantrap clams). The mantrap clam is two feet or more in diameter when fully grown and can hold a man under if he should be so unlucky as to get an arm or leg caught, but we went only after the babies. How delicious the meat was, fresh from the polished white shells. And pity the fish that snooped around us, for it was immediately grabbed and eaten raw.

The scent of blood attracted the striped, lizard-like fish that stubbornly picked at our cuts. We tried to kick them or lure them away by throwing meat to a distant point, but the little rascals kept coming back, to pick and nibble at our food and at us.

A fish carnival was in progress at the bottom of the lagoon. Majestic columns of bluish cavallas swam by above the open-mouthed mantrap clams on their bright coral beds. There were "angel fish," with their extended decorative streamers hanging from their lower fins, and our friends the tiny-mouthed "balloon fish," which filled their bladders with air and at the slightest sign of danger floated to the surface for us to play with.

Occasionally a white shark would disrupt the fun by suddenly darting toward us, his always present pilot fish seemingly attached to his bleached, pale belly. But as suddenly as he appeared Mr. Shark would vanish, being interested in more serious matters.

We had little fear of sharks in the lagoon, for at the slightest hint of danger from a too businesslike shark we would either swim to the nearest high coral, and there were many coral heads close by, or pound the sea with our feet and fists to frighten the fellow away. But usually the sharks ignored us completely, wishing to investigate quarry that did not make so much noise.

And we hardly thought of danger when we saw a sting ray gliding steadily along the bottom, spooning clayish white sand with his powerful revolving wings, a sword of a tail dragging behind. Papa, at the sight of him, cautioned us to be still, so as not to irritate the sting ray while he was searching the bottom for food.

When we had spent a full half day in the lagoon we gathered some *pauas* to take home with us for a chowder dinner. It took us an hour to swim back to the beach.

After such a long time in the water and sun we children were so tired that in the afternoon we dozed in the shade of our lean-to, while Papa, his inspiration returned, worked on *Amaru*. Then, before dinner, we all took another swim. But this time for barely an hour.

CHAPTER 22

A South Sea White Man

*I am fond of the toddlers, but this is not sloppy sentiment.
I do not enjoy kissing them, petting them, talking to them in
the so-called language of infants. I feel genuine concern over
their troubles, and I watch them develop with interest and
amusement. I find a certain crafty pleasure in devising methods
by which they can be trained in such a way that they enjoy
being trained, and at the same time I am not overfatigued.*

(Letter to James Norman Hall.)

How can I describe the fun and joy we all shared?

Walking through the coconut grove with the dark blue ocean
and the iridescent lagoon both visible on each side, we might
see a white baby tern perched on a pandanus tree, in its cosy
grass nest. One by one we would climb carefully toward the
bird to whisper very softly, *"Noo akalelei e taku, manu
mengiti,"* meaning , "Sit prettily, my little bird," or "Your life
be happy, my little bird." It is the same as saying "Good night"
and "Good-by" in Puka-Pukan.

There were times when the four of us broke away from Papa's hands to vanish like untamed animals among the maires (ferns). He was a clever man. Because he could not hear the rattling of dried coconut fronds that were laid on the path so lovers at night could find their way to the beach, he suspected this to be a game. So he stopped, looked at the tamanu trees, untied and refastened his faded red *pareu,* mumbled in English, "Someday I shall build myself a little house in a tree where you kids won't be able to bother me."

Then turning to "discover" our absence, he called, "Hey, kids, where are you?"

Like a cautious hunter, Papa searched everywhere: under the dried coconut leaves, in the scented ferns, on the low *Puka* (hernandia) and pandanus trees (for he had yet to master the art of climbing tall trees). And when he thought he saw something he screamed, "There you are, you little lizard!" Only it was an old tree stump.

My! But that was a good game, especially when he walked toward our hide-out, brushing aside the leaves, looking under the fronds, and sometimes sitting unsuspectingly next to a hiding body to rest. He must have known he was sitting close to someone, but he conspired with us shivering children to build up the excitement before the discovery.

The ride on a coconut tree trunk which had fallen halfway to the ground was the most fun of all! We ran ahead of Papa and climbed the leaning tree in readiness.

"Please, Papa," we asked in English, the few words that we knew.

"Ready, set, go!" down went the tree, then up a little way. Down again, and up some more. Then down very fast, and high, high, high up again, way above the shrubbery. Then as the leaning tree moved faster and faster, our hearts began to beat more rapidly; our feet and arms were wrapped tightly around the tree.

"Enough?" Papa would ask.

"Yes! Please, yes!" we screamed. "Ohhh, my head, my head is dizzy, Papa. That was really good! Oh, thank you. *E apinga meitaki tikai teia* [This is wonderful]!"

After the ride we ran as fast as we could, gasping for that cool ocean water to wash away the heat from our excited bodies. Arriving underneath the big *taeyinu* tree that shaded the pool, the four of us took our clothes off and climbed as high as we could, seeking a place that was thick with leaves, which no one could possibly discover except the slippery small lizards and industrious ants. There, at the very top, we perched like long-necked birds, heads above the young leaves, watching excitedly for Papa to come looking for us.

"The clothes are here; they must be in the water." He spoke loudly, walking around the pool, opening his eyes even wider as he searched the clear and untouched water. At times he turned big stones and tipped over little shells, as if he might find bodies hiding, muttering, "Now where could they be? Up in the tree-top, maybe?"

Then our four pairs of eyes popped wide open as Papa attempted to climb an easy tree, asked a busy army of ants where he could find four little ones, looked disgustedly at them because they did not answer, and said, "You, too, little ants, won't get any of my lollipops." At this rare offer the branches moved! Dry leaves fell to the ground and little branches cracked and fell as four naked children descended hurriedly, yelling, "Papa! Wait! Wait for us!"

"No, no, no," he yelled back, running toward the pool, at the same time untying his *pareu* and allowing it to fall carelessly to the ground.

"Papa! No! Wait for us!"

He was never caught, although he was a slow runner, because his four pursuers refused to let him be caught. We, too, were actors, trying to look as if we were running fast, yet taking short strides.

CHAPTER 23

Uninhabited Suwarrow

Now and again we discover a man who has had the good fortune or the courage to change completely his way of life: The haberdasher jumps a freight, the greengrocer goes to war, the burglar becomes a hairdresser; and when this occurs we see, as it were, an oyster emerge from its shell, a fossil burst from its rock stratum. The man's eyes become alight with a sort of spiritual surprise; he discovers that life is still worth the living; he finds interest in youth, old books, new drinks, the chorus. Sometimes he sows a belated crop of wild oats: sometimes he becomes a philanthropist, a bad poet, a cabinet minister; but whatever he does his work fills him with delight, which in turn is passed on to his fellow man.

But how prone most of us are to destroy the spirit so long as the body may be established permanently in sloth and security. Henri Bergson showed how evolution ceases when a creature develops a hard shell or some other natural defense; and Bergson might have added . . . "or when a creature buys a house and lot or settles on a South Sea Island." It seems that the Author of all things is obliged to visit men with terrible disasters, like the present war, to force them to refresh their languid spirits through material change. For when a man changes his way of life he is reborn spiritually: though he retain the wisdom of years he sees life through the clear and unprejudiced eyes of childhood; and even his material self is rejuvenated by some potent elixir passed from the spirit to the body.

Probably most men experience this spiritual regeneracy at marriage or at the death of a parent; but then, unless they be fortunate indeed, they settle in a steady and comfortable vehicle, pull down the blinds, and jog along languidly toward the physical death that is only an unimportant afterpart of the spiritual death, which last has already been solemnized.

(Letter from Papa to his brother, April 16, 1942.)

At the height of one of Papa's periods of restlessness he decided to take the family on a "world tour" of the islands of the South Pacific. On the day Papa told us of his plans for the trip, I walked through the village of Yato, calling my friends to tell them of the news. It was just a few days after Christmas of 1941. I could not find anyone, and concluded that my friends had already heard the news and gone to hide because they were hurt and did not want to see me again. I stopped in front of Cousin Tili's house, dejectedly calling her name.

"*E, Tili-ariki!* I have true news today! We are leaving Puka-Puka on the next boat. I'm not lying; please come out and listen to me."

I finally gave up and went to Mama Tala's house. She, after hearing my words, wailed just as she had when her mother, Tangi, had died. She fell to her knees and started chanting Mama's name in self-torture. She felt that it would be a long time before she would ever see us again, maybe never.

The news that we were leaving created a near revolution on

this tiny island. Mama's relatives spread the idea that Papa was doing wrong in taking us away from Puka-Puka, the only island worth living on, and they threatened to kidnap us. Their threats were not made directly to Papa, but to other relatives, each hoping that Papa might hear of them and reconsider. Few of our well-intentioned relatives were brave enough to approach Papa directly, but those who were, after a few muttered words from a memorized speech, were likely to hear him bellow, "Get the hell out of here or I'll never give you any more tobacco."

After a few days our relatives reversed their attitude and with typical Polynesian generosity started loading us up with mats, hats, sennits, and other departing gifts. It is a rare islander who can for many days maintain a feud or any other kind of unpleasantness. Our relatives visited us almost every night, sitting cross-legged in our living room, discussing with Papa subjects of common interest: the weather, fishing, and new babies. Papa, in turn, discoursed on the broadening aspects of travel and dispensed twisted tobacco and matches to all.

When the cutter *Typee* arrived to take us away, the whole island came down to Yato Beach to see us off. It was not a happy crowd. A weird, undulating wail could be heard at times from the multitude of relatives and friends. Even the men who shook Papa's hands shed tears. Mama Tala hung onto the four of us, wrapping her fat arms around us and bringing to my mind the sad scene of Mama bidding farewell to Papa when he went away to America a few years before. Mama had cried bitterly and later became seriously ill. Now Mama Tala was crying and saying, "I know you'll not come back."

Leaving Puka-Puka on the *Typee* late that stormy afternoon for the little uninhabited island of Suwarrow, some two hundred and fifty miles to the southeast, we lost sight of land when we were scarcely two miles out at sea. The breakers were un-

believably high, so that only spray marked where land had
been. We cried, thinking that Puka-Puka had sunk, but Papa
consoled us.

"Now, now, kids, Puka-Puka is still floating around back
there and will be when we return."

The trip lasted a week. We spent nearly all of it on deck
because it smelled so bad below. When it rained, we pulled
a tarpaulin over us—and enjoyed the sound of raindrops landing upon the tough cloth. When we needed to go to the w.c.
we simply perched on the side of the boat, holding onto the
iron railing.

We ate the same breakfast every morning. It was a gooey
cereal dish of a texture not unlike thousands of tiny wet fish
eyes. Every night we feasted on boiled albacores and coconuts.
We drank only tea, since the "fresh" water tasted strongly
of the rust in the old tanks.

The voyage took considerably more than the normal sailing time because twice during the trip the *Typee* lost the wind
and rolled helplessly on her barnacle-covered belly, waiting
for a breeze to blow. During these calms we swam away from
the boat, filled with the ecstasy of the lovely, quiet sea.

Very early one morning we raised the first outlying islet of
Suwarrow Atoll. But it was not until noon that we anchored
close to the submerged pier at lonely Anchorage Island.

"We'll stop here for a while, cowboys," our father announced.

After making arrangements with Captain Cambridge to
pick us up in four months on his return trip, Papa gave us
orders to unload the gear and follow him inland by an unused
path. He set off at a fast pace, and seemed to know exactly
where he was going.

Carrying bundles of clothes, food, cooking utensils, and his
writing equipment, we made our way through the young

coconut trees, the thick maire groves, busy with hermit and land crabs, and the giant *tou* trees, their bright orange blossoms scattered by the sea wind among the birds' nests in the nearby *taeyinu* trees.

Jakey, Elaine, Nga, and I stopped halfway before reaching the tamanu grove, where we were to build our shelter, telling Papa that we wanted to stay behind a minute and have a short conference. He did not object to this, for it was quite common for us to have meetings without him. We watched him disappear down the trail, his thin, tanned legs poking out of patched khaki pants and sweat running down his bare back. A typewriter swung in one hand, a bundle of clothes in the other, and he had a fish pole and fish line under his arms. "Papa looks like a tangled-up coconut crab," announced Jakey.

He melted away in the suddenly lonely jungle, the branches folding back in place, as if purposely trying to conceal him.

Calming our fears at being left alone on a strange island, we began the meeting with the understanding that we would leave Papa alone for a while, so that he could have time to reminisce about the period, several years before, when Mama, Jakey, and I had visited Suwarrow. Then we agreed it would be best not to disagree with Papa's suggestions concerning a good location to build our little shack. "And we should never, never fight! Just be patient," little Nga told the others.

"*E, e.*" We nodded in approval.

We then planned a program. First, Jakey must climb coconut trees and cut down enough fronds for the roof of our new home; not sit around with his mouth open, waiting for Papa to tell him what to do. "Be on the alert," I reminded him. Next, Elaine and Nga must diligently clean the area around our new home and gather the firewood. I was to stay with Papa as his aide while we put up the house, which would take about a day.

"Ei aa tatou e tamaki," Nga repeated, as Papa sometimes did, when he didn't want us to fight.

"You remember that yourself!" Elaine retorted.

"Okay!" Nga agreed with great emphasis, showing us that she was capable of keeping peace in the family.

We looked at her and smiled. It's wonderful to take orders from a *potiki.*

These meetings of ours often prevented trouble later, for we were not such sweet, agreeable sisters and brother as we seemed to be to others. We had very few bad fights, but had as many arguments as there are starfish in the ocean, and often our meetings were no more than slightly organized quarrels. But we did not think our arguments were bad. They were quite interesting, even if Papa thought the opposite.

Once Papa sketched ugly caricatures to show how we looked when we sneered, grumbled, and snarled at each other. This system worked with Elaine, Nga, and me, for we did not appreciate his sketches at all. But Jakey just laughed hysterically at the drawings, until he complained of a pain in his side.

We followed the untrodden path till we found Papa in an open clearing among the coconuts and tamanus.

There was a well filled with dirty green rain water under an old corrugated iron roof. The white gravel scattered around the well, covered with leaves and crumbling branches, had turned a greenish gray from the dampness. The place had a strong smell of decay. But it was not an unpleasant odor, and we soon became used to it.

We expected to discover Papa sitting on one of the coconut tree stumps half in tears, dreaming of the past. Instead he was busy clearing away old leaves, rocks, and land crabs that had built their homes around the well. We wondered if he was ashamed to be caught crying, for we knew Mama was there with him at that moment.

We built our house in record time. Jakey, remembering his instructions, climbed the tall coconut trees to cut down the fronds. The steps he took as he ascended the trees were well timed, as if he were measuring his strides with the beat of some invisible drum, audible only to himself. Even the fronds fell to the ground rhythmically, to the cadence of his chopping blade. Elaine and I gathered and plaited the fallen fronds where they fell. Nga dragged the finished products to Papa, who was chopping up trees and measuring them for posts. We laughed at her because she counted every step she took. Soon we were digging holes and planting the posts. Papa and Jakey climbed to the top of the skeleton house; Elaine and I handed them sticks and the plaited fronds for the roof. When this was done, we made baskets to take to the opposite side of the island, to gather white gravel for the floor of our beautiful new home. It was nightfall, and the house, although needing a few touches here and there, was ready to live in.

As the moon rose, we undressed by the well, rushed down to the beach, and frightened the peaceful fish away with our splashing. Now they would have company every day, three times a day, and we knew that soon they would get tired of the tumultuous water and move away in disgust, blowing bubbles as their way of showing their displeasure.

It was at Suwarrow that we discovered how easily Papa could fit into the life of the wilderness. He did not have bulging muscles, but he cut down the largest branches from the tamanu trees without trouble. He might have looked a little awkward climbing, but soon he was up there building his own tree house in the highest branches so he could write, away from our chatter. He was a much better fisherman than we. He knew what bait and hook would fool the shark, that a live *kaloma* is an ulua's favorite dish, and that a mashed hermit crab will certainly arouse a *tarao's* hunger. And he knew how to make the most of the native food available: he made excellent biscuits from grated coconut and flour, and delicious and heavenly-smelling bread from flour and *uto*.

One afternoon, not long after we were settled in our new home, we children went hunting hermit crabs for bait. They are the best bait for catching lagoon fish, because not only do they have a powerful odor but they are also tasty. We knew, for to properly prepare the crab for bait we would chew it to a pulp.

Papa had gone for a walk, and since we wanted to surprise him we went to the windward side of the island, which he seldom visited. We soon were crawling under the lanky roots of pandanus trees, snatching the red hermit crabs from their hiding places and stuffing them into empty coconut shells. It was late in the afternoon when we finished, and we hurried home, hoping that Papa was not already there, for we wanted to have the catch ready when he walked in the door. We arranged the shells on the floor, and the waiting period began.

Time dragged by, and our gay talk faded to silence. It became dusk, then dark, and with it came an eerie quietness that struck our hearts with fear. The only sound came from the imprisoned crabs, rustling in their coconut shells. We began to cry, blaming each other for letting Papa go alone into the bushes. Maybe a dried coconut had fallen on his head. Maybe a shark had eaten him when he went for a short swim, as he usually did each afternoon. Or, even worse, maybe a ghost had strangled him. We cried louder, hoping that Papa would hear us and come running home.

By seven o'clock we had quite given up hope of ever seeing Papa again, when we heard the rattling of leaves and the familiar tune of his whistling. Wiping our eyes, we quickly sat up in a row, hands on our knees, smiles taking the place of tears. He came to the door, looked at us in a surprised manner, and said, "Hey! I thought you were still out looking for crabs!"

"No, Papa," we answered in harmony.

We showed him our crabs, not telling him how frightened we had been, and Papa told us we were all going on a fishing and exploring trip the next day.

"Those crabs will certainly come in handy, cowboys," he said. "That really solves a big problem. Now we'll catch plenty of fish tomorrow!" We felt happy and useful.

Before retiring we lit a small fire and sat around it. The night had grown cloudy, but we could still see the breakers on the reef. Papa told us another story of Ulysses and his travels. I pictured myself as that great hero, and dreamed of one day sailing *Panikiniki* through the Mediterranean, from Troy to the gates of the Hellespont. I wished that Ulysses were still alive so that I could meet him and perhaps ask him to visit Puka-Puka and Suwarrow.

The next morning very early we carried *Panikiniki* to the beach. We had brought her with us on the *Typee,* for we could not part with her.

Papa looked at the sky and said, "It's going to rain soon."

"Yes, and it's a good thing we brought *Panikiniki* with us, heh, Papa?" Nga asked as we carried the little canoe from under the protection of the trees.

"You're right, a very good thing!"

"Papa," Elaine asked, "what if we didn't?"

"Well, we'd have to make another just like her."

"Oh?" Then looking at Papa, Elaine said in a very low voice, "Papa, you can't make a canoe, can you?"

"Sure! I made that little canoe in Yato."

Again Elaine looked at him with an innocent distrust. "Papa, *you* didn't make that canoe."

"Elaine, do you think I would lie to you?"

Elaine wanted to say "Yes," but shook her head.

The instant we hoisted *Panikiniki's* sail it shook the canoe, as if playing a game with the wind. Papa steered into the huge lagoon, away from land and straight toward the cloudy horizon. We watched the long line of the wake, and could measure the tremendous speed by it. We asked why Papa steered the canoe away from the visible island, but he shook his head and shrugged his shoulders, meaning for us to mind our business and let him do the navigating. He liked to surprise us. So we sang and whistled for the wind to blow harder. It did, and the waves rose higher, too, giving Jakey and me that great opportunity of sitting together on the outrigger boom. We sailed farther away from our island home and watched it disappear in a rain squall. I wondered if we would ever find it again; I did not see how we could.

Soon we were in the middle of the lagoon. A lagoon full of man-eating sharks, I thought. It was not like our lagoon on Puka-Puka, for it was so deep we could not see the colorful corals blooming below, with which we were so familiar.

The canoe kept on its own course for nowhere; the raindrops were too heavy for us to see land. Jakey yelled at Papa, asking where we were going. Papa pointed his finger and over the wind yelled the magic words, "Motu Tou." Then we realized we were going to visit his favorite island, where all the giant *tou* trees grew, the type of tree from which he had made beautiful trays and book ends. Papa once said that if trunks of this tree were kept two years in water a boat could be built to last longer than life itself.

"Papa, why do you sail toward the center of the lagoon when you really mean to sail to one of the islands around the reef?" Elaine asked when the wind had fallen off a little.

"My foolish children, if you were good sailors you would know that we cannot sail straight to Motu Tou because the wind is directly in front, so we must sail to the center of the lagoon, then to Motu Tou on the reef. This is called tacking. Now if we wanted to go to Turtle Island we wouldn't have to sail so far before we tacked. Do you know why? Because Turtle Island is much closer than Motu Tou. Now figure that out, and if you think you don't understand let's talk some more."

We gave a sign that we understood. Even Nga, who we knew did not understand a word Papa had said, vigorously nodded her little head.

After several hours on the choppy water and beneath the splattering raindrops we sighted Motu Tou, with its dwarf coconut trees along the beach hiding the trunks of the taller trees further inland. We opened our eyes wider to see frigate and white kaka birds perching under shelter, wings covering their heads to protect them from the rain. Shielding our eyes, we searched for a place to land. We could not imagine how we would be able to walk inland once we had landed, the trees were so thick and the bushes so tightly packed. Papa yelled to lower the sail. Before *Panikiniki's* belly scraped the sand, Jakey, Elaine, Nga, and I jumped overboard for a refreshing swim, hanging onto the sides and letting the canoe carry us ashore.

In the water we saw the scattered bones of giant whales. We wanted to dig up some pieces to take home. But since we were always gathering old bottles, interesting pieces of rusted iron, and sea shells, Papa strongly objected to our carrying around a ten-foot jawbone for a souvenir.

The scratching noise of countless crabs crawling on the beach and in the bushes came to us as we carried *Panikiniki* onto the smooth beach. Here and there brown land crabs scurried under rotten tree stumps, leaves, or coconut husks, eating anything available. Very seldom during the day do these landlubbers crawl to the beach to bathe. Hundreds of white sand crabs, with brown freckles on their backs and claws, dug their holes in the sand even faster as we came near them. They live on seaweed and dead fish, and seldom go inland, where life is too complicated for their simple beachcomber habits. And when they do wander inland, they rarely return to their beautiful beach.

"Jakey, you're a big *ropa;* why don't you carry the sail?"

"Papa!" we gasped, knowing this meant that we were to spend the night on this uninhabited, ghostlike, and mysterious island. *"Aue, aue! Te mataku e* [Oh, oh! How scary this place is]!"

We filled our arms with whatever we could carry, asked Papa which direction to take, then hurried on ahead, now and again sitting under the trees to wait for him or climbing a tall tree to watch him casually and unconcernedly walking below, his thoughts probably far away. If we wanted his attention we squeaked like birds or grunted like pigs. We had never heard a cow moo or a horse neigh, so we could not try to scare him in these ways.

Papa pointed out to us a magnificent strip of land, narrow, with white sandbanks rising quite high, almost four feet above sea level. The day was clearing, and as the sun broke through the clouds the beautiful sand reflected the light, blinding us a little. But when the lazy waves washed ashore, the sand would dull for a moment and then blaze once again with the hot sunlight. It was a windy spot, pleasingly so to the white terns perched on *taeyinu* trees. There was no doubt that we would enjoy camping here.

Papa fashioned a cozy tent from the sail by laying it over a branch. We gathered coconut fronds and placed these around the edges of the sail in an upright form, to protect us from the wind at night. For a mattress we spread freshly dried leaves, and over them laid split coconut fronds. I remember with delight how soft and very crunchy the bed was. There were three big trees surrounding the little area to protect us from the strong northerly wind. There were grass nests in these trees for the baby kakas and white tern eggs on the bare branches. We shall sleep with the birds tonight, I thought.

That night, we ate roasted birds that crackled a little on the burning coal, baked crabs with dripping fat that almost drowned the fire, tasty *utos*, and sweet coconut juice.

We watched the half-moon and speculated on where the other half was. Elaine loved the crescent moon, for it reminded her of the shape of her beloved bananas. We sang songs to Mama, as we often did at night, and much later crawled into our tent, which Papa called a "wigwam."

The next morning, we awakened early, even before the birds, washed our ears and eyes in the clear fresh sea water from the reef nearby, and ate breakfast of baked birds' eggs and *utos* with coconut juice.

Standing on the edge of the reef with fishing rods in our hands, sitting on rocks inside the reef, or poking our heads into little holes to look for fish and sea shells, we also hunted little *mokaras* (ducks) in search of their favorite insects and worms. The strong Suwarrow sun burned our bare and oiled backs. If one of us detected something of interest he would yell, "Papa, come and see this! Hurry, Papa, hurry!" Elaine, at one time, found something and called for Papa in a squealing voice, waving her hands, wiggling her body, and slapping at the wind for disturbing the water.

"What is it? What is it, Elaine? Is it a big one? Is it a fish?" Papa yelled excitedly, as he attempted to run on the rocks without slipping on the seaweed or black *roris* (sea slugs).

Jakey and I watched Papa look into the small hole for at least ten minutes, trying to see a very conspicuous little eel, pretending that he could not see it. He rubbed his eyes, stuck his posterior up in the air, and spread his legs wide as he practically kissed the surface of the water looking for the eel.

"Elaine, I can't see a thing! Where is it? What is it? Why do you always play tricks on me?"

"Papa, *tena, tena!*" Elaine pointed impatiently.

"Where? I can't see a thing. Oh, Elaine, you must be blind. That's no eel at all. It's just a little helpless *rori.*"

"Papa!" Elaine took his hand in exasperation and placed it above the eel. "Right there, look! And it is *not* a sea slug!"

With a loud yell of excitement and surprise Papa sat on the shallow reef. "Oh, my! It's the biggest eel I've seen all week. Did you chase it here all by yourself? Johnny, Jakey, Nga, come and see the eel Elaine found!" Elaine's face was like that of a proud Puka-Pukan wrestler after a great triumph.

Thus passed a happy week on Motu Tou. In the morning we fished from the unexplored reefs, sitting on the coral rocks to eat the raw fish we had caught, then plunged into the reef pools to swim and later, drying in the sun, talked of Mama, asking Papa to tell us more of her. We searched for her favorite periwinkles and sea shells and unusual fish. In the afternoons we explored the land, crawling under thick trees or climbing over them. We stoned kakas for dinner by throwing small rocks at them and lit coconut torches to poke into hollowed trees, to flush out the tasty coconut crabs.

Once when it rained, we gathered into the hollowed trunk of a hernandia tree for protection. It was dark inside, and Papa lit a match. There, next to Elaine's muddy foot, was a skull many years old. In the shocked silence Papa announced that the rest of the body must have been carried away by crabs. We four jumped out into the rain, lips quivering from fear, eyes frantically looking in every direction, to be on guard for the dead man's ghost. But if there was a ghost, it was friendly that night and did not bother us.

Sometimes in the early evening we would stroll the beaches, picking up driftwood or glass balls that had floated many miles from mysterious Japan.

At night we sang our favorite songs for Mama and slept soundly. When we sailed away from Motu Tou we felt as if we were leaving home, but Anchorage Island beckoned us to return. Papa sensed a strangeness in the air, and we helped the stiff sail with our paddles.

CHAPTER 24

The Hurricane

A big storm on a low atoll may be very serious, so we always watch the weather closely during this time of the year, and we heave rather large sighs when March is over and the winds come from the Trade quarter again, the southeast.

(Papa's letter to his mother, February 1935.)

The first power of the February hurricane of 1942 came at nightfall of the twenty-first. A strong gust of wind, followed by the sharp, pellet-like raindrops from a low scudding cloud, pulled at the trees much as an archer might tentatively test his bow before notching an arrow.

A hush fell over the thirteen of us huddled closely in the corrugated iron shack which was the largest building on the island. All were men with the exception of Elaine, Nga, and myself. There were the three New Zealand weathermen; their three Manihikian helpers; Ronald Powell and John Pratt, who had anchored in Suwarrow Lagoon two days earlier on the yacht *Vagus*; and the five of us. It was a square room, with a wireless radio. The radio stuttered and played annoying tricks. Try as we would, we could decipher no weather information from the station. The wireless operator slapped and and swore at it and called the radio a worthless box of rubbish. At one time he lifted it and threatened to throw it out the closed window.

"Listen to me!" Papa said, and he had to scream because the wind by now was blowing strong against the coconut shutters on the wall. Pointing to his calculations on the map, he told us that the strong northeasterly wind must be headed for Suwarrow. He said that if the wind was a hurricane we were in a bad position on Suwarrow because we would be right smack in its path. Just then the radio cleared for a spell and we heard that Puka-Puka was at that moment being hit by the worst hurricane in years but had no casualities so far. I cried for Mama Tala, seeing in my mind the little sleeping house only a few feet from the water.

Fear was on the faces of several of us as we looked about the flimsy room and listened to the mounting wind. But Papa seemed exhilarated by the advance of this hurricane. He looked forward to it as material he could write about. Already he could picture himself telling Hall how it was to experience a *real* hurricane. The wind blew stronger and fiercer. Suddenly the roof of the house came off with a strangely subdued tearing sound, and we were forced to abandon the room and run for our lives to our house under the tamanu trees. It was a tight fit, but everyone managed to squeeze in. Then we waited. Just before midnight Papa forced himself out into the storm to visit his tree house, where he kept all his books, writing papers, and his ancient Remington typewriter. He took along a bottle of rum and some tobacco. When he returned he was smiling, and came over to sit by us. He asked Ronald Powell to station himself in the doorway to watch for the high waves.

The three New Zealanders sat crouched in a corner, fear

in their eyes, not saying a word. They held tight to the ropes around their waists, which could be tied around a coconut tree if they found themselves in rising water. Papa had shown us how to use these ropes. We were to tie them around a tree so that the rising sea could carry us up and down but never out to the ocean toward the reef or to the deep water in the lagoon. If we felt that the coconut tree was falling, then we were to free the ends of the rope and swim for another tree. The only trouble was, Papa said, half the trees were already uprooted by the sea. On his trip to the tree house he had been forced to dodge branches and debris which, along with the uprooted trees, were piled high on the center of the island. Even the giant tamanu trees had no chance of survival against the combined force of the wind and the waves. They seemed to give up life easily and slide down into the hungry water. But the five tamanus growing close together by our house stood proudly and refused defeat. Their roots held tight even when the sea dug deep and washed away the soil that covered them.

The breakers, however, continued to increase in size, and at two o'clock in the morning, while we were fitfully dozing, Powell, who was on watch, yelled even louder than the wind:

"Look out! A wave's coming!"

It was too late to stand. The wave crashed through the door and washed us in a heap against the side of the house. The water was up to our necks. It quickly receded, apparently losing its force among the trees. Papa grabbed Elaine's hand and squatted so that Nga could jump onto his back. He ordered Jakey and me to follow him to the pearling cutter.

"Hurry! Hurry, kids! We have no time to lose!"

The others had gone, and we suspected they were in the tree house. The cutter that Papa had tied to a tree was still afloat, a tarpaulin over it keeping out the rain. We had no trouble seeing our way, thanks to the continual flashes of lightning. We climbed into the pearling cutter and waited. Papa tried to smoke a damp cigarette rolled in a pandanus leaf while he gave us instructions. We were to stay close at all times, and if we were washed to sea we must reach for objects that might pull us back. "Please, yell, scream, so that I'll know where to find you. But I know you'll need little or no help."

It was while Papa was calming us by kissing our cheeks that a comber crashed against the cutter, turning it over and instantly throwing us into the swirling water. Elaine and Nga hung onto Papa, who just managed to keep his head above the sea. Jakey was lost to sight, but we could hear him yelling, "Papa! Papa!" as he struggled against the backwash. I had gone over with the cutter, but swam under and away from it. As I emerged, a corrugated iron plank from the cookhouse came hurtling toward me. I just had time to duck under again and let the plank go over me. Then I swam toward Papa, bumping into Jakey on the way. We held hands as the wave angrily receded and crawled to the five tamanu trees, fighting the wind that seemed to want to lift us off the ground. Papa was dazed with shock, and swore at the top of his lungs at the other men for having left him alone with us. But he quickly pulled himself together and yelled at us, "Hurry! Hurry, before another wave comes!"

As he himself recalled in *The Island of Desire:* "I tied Elaine on my back again and this time took Nga under my arm, for the tamanus were to windward, and Johnny could not carry her sister against the wind. We crawled past the tank on our hands and knees, seeming to force our heads and shoulders into a solid substance, feeling our bodies too light to grip the ground. It was slow work and it was desperate work, for constantly we were haunted by the knowledge that we might not reach the trees before the next sea came. Even now it makes a cold sweat start from my skin when I recall that laborious half hour's struggle when the five of us wormed painfully through the solid body of wind, desperate but not despairing. Brave children! They dug their toes and fingers in the sand and pushed forward like draft horses hauling a heavy load. And the seas! The seas! Would another comber rage through the clearing before we made the tamanus?"

Papa placed me in a natural basket formed by a fork in the trunk of one of the five tamanus. Then he gave Nga to Powell, who lashed himself onto another tree. Jakey and Elaine crawled with Papa to the tree house on the third tree. But Papa did not sit and relax. He stood in the doorway of the house, watching me in my tree and Ronald Powell and Nga in theirs. He was ready to come to us in case of trouble. During the next few hours Papa cut down two huge branches threatening to fall on the tree house. I had never been so proud of him. He stood against the trunk of the tree, leaning toward the wind, over twenty feet above the ground, chopping with the ax and wiping the salted raindrops that stung his face.

When this was finished, I saw him give Elaine and Jakey a drink of rum to warm their blood. Then, clinging to roots and branches and clutching the bottle against his stomach, he crawled over to Nga and Powell to give them a sip of rum also. When he reached me at my tree he missed by a second a comber that would have washed him away forever. He was so frightened I had to hold him steady, and when he looked up at me his eyes were watery and happy. He must have been thinking of this moment when he wrote: "It terrifies me to anticipate what might happen in a state of delirium—or what might happen were I to die! Think of these four children, age four to ten, left alone on Suwarrow Atoll!"

When he left, I did not see him again until after the wind

had subsided and the waves had changed their course. When he returned for me in the late afternoon he was a little tipsy from the rum and in pain from an attack of filarial fever. He carried me to a tent where the rest of the children were already asleep on wet pandanus mats and brown woolen blankets. As his fever increased, I searched in vain among the rubbish for morphine or quinine. The bottles were broken and the medicine lost or soaked.

That night, Papa moaned in pain and cried loud for medicine to ease his suffering. We cuddled very close to him to keep his body warm, and held him down when he blindly fought to get up. He wanted us to let him go so that he could run into the still tossing sea. "Let me die! Let me die!" he pleaded. We knew he was out of his mind, driven into madness by the fever.

During the next ten days, the sun was hidden by clouds and occasional rain. We took care of Papa and fed him hot coconut meat and juice, raw fish, and broiled albatrosses. For his birthday, April 16, we children gathered cigarette stubs that had been thrown about by the New Zealanders. Then we killed several white tropical birds and plucked the long, thin, golden feathers from their tails. These we exchanged with the New Zealanders for two unsmoked cigarettes. On the sixteenth we took the tobacco out of the stubs and wrapped it in a young coconut leaf. We placed the two beautiful whole cigarettes beside it in a hiding place in the bushes. Then we ran to find Papa. He was up now and typing, but he stopped when we asked him to play a game with us and follow an Indian trail that we had made. He followed the directions of the pointed rocks, the arrows on the sand, and was led to the hidden presents. We could see he was truly surprised and pleased, but all he said was, "I didn't think you'd remember this was my birthday."

Our relations with the New Zealanders quickly deteriorated. One day they asked us children to help salvage goods in the mounds of debris left by the hurricane. There were piles of chipped coral and boulders, broken coconut fronds, dead albatrosses, terns, and wide-awake birds, beached sharks and groupers, and clawless, headless coconut crabs. We searched the rubbish for tins of fruit and meat. The New Zealanders demanded that we give them anything we found other than our own possessions. We did return to them several cans of fruit, corned beef, salmon, and some soggy packages of Jello, but we hid some in the sand for ourselves. When we returned to our cache that night, the food had disappeared. We found that the three frightened weathermen suspected us, and so to be certain that they were not being cheated returned in the late afternoon to re-examine the places we had worked.

We were very angry with them, not appreciating the fact that these men had less chance of surviving on Suwarrow than we had. They could not eat raw birds and crabs. They did not know how to fish without civilized equipment and made no attempt to learn. The only native food they were able to find was green coconuts and the older, sprouted coconuts. Once or twice they ate broiled fish we had caught and exchanged with them for a rusty tin of beef. We wanted to share our food with them, but they insisted on hoarding every tin they owned before the storm. Papa built a lean-to with salvaged sheet iron which would catch the rain water, but the New Zealanders demanded that Papa return the iron roofs. So Papa made another rain catch for our family out of a sail which had been buried in the sand.

This was a fortunate discovery, for it led us to find our old friend *Panikiniki* close by. We dug her out and soon had her ready to sail again.

The only part of the atoll left intact was Turtle Island, for the other islands were completely stripped of their foliage and were now nothing but barren sandcays. Turtle Island was some five miles north of Anchorage. The center of this island had not been touched by the sea, but the coconut trees were bare of nuts. We gathered fallen nuts and captured huge coconut crabs, who in their lazy isolation had grown fat on the surplus of fruits and nuts left on the ground. We sailed back to Anchorage Island with *Panikiniki* well packed with food, sitting high on piles of coconuts, crabs, and fish.

One day the New Zealanders asked to borrow *Panikiniki* to sail to Turtle Island to gather coconuts. We hoped our relations would improve if we let them use the canoe, so Papa agreed. Emptying the canoe on their return, they wound the rope around a small rock. Soon poor *Panikiniki* started drifting away. Papa swam after her, but the sharks were so numerous in the lagoon he returned. He marched dripping-wet to the New Zealanders' tent and in a loud and angry voice demanded in exchange for the loss of our canoe a dozen cans of milk, the same of corned beef, half a kerosene can of flour, sugar, and coffee. He reminded them of their stupidity and inconsideration and stinginess. And Papa told them that if the aforementioned articles were not delivered to us by sundown he was going to return to the tent and kill all three of them! This ultimatum delivered, he returned to our hut and wrote a scathing letter to the New Zealand Government, to send whenever a ship chanced to sail to Suwarrow. But we knew that this letter would be forgotten by nightfall as Papa was the type who forgave easily.

Before sundown the New Zealanders sent us supplies of food. We ate well until two months later, when the *Tagua* sailed into the lagoon to take us to Manihiki.

CHAPTER 25

Manihiki: Wife Number Two

In the deepening twilight I will lead you
To a lonely secret place.
There no man's eye will see you;
We shall flee through curtaining clouds
And nest in the farthest heavens.
(Puka-Pukan love chant, page 62, THE BOOK OF PUKA-PUKA.)

The last time I visited Manihiki was before Mama and I were married," Papa said as we stood on the deck of the schooner *Tagua*, clad in tattered *pareus* of such ragged appearance that anybody might correctly guess we had just been rescued from an uninhabited island.

"I think this is the most beautiful island of them all. And the women here are as lovely as their island. They are so beautiful that in the past one of their greatest dangers was being kidnaped by sailors. Wait until you see them. I think that I shall look around for a wife here."

We left Papa dreaming by the rail and walked to the forward deck, passing the galley, where the cook was broiling coffee

beans. The smell of roasting coffee always makes the mouth
water, particularly in the early morning. We walked over half-
asleep pigs that lazily wiggled and twitched their nostrils as
if they, too, desired a cup of steaming coffee. There were
chickens, also, well packed in crates. The stench was powerful,
worse than that of Suwarrow after the hurricane, when the dead
fish, birds, and crabs had rotted.

We sat on the bowsprit, watching the people gather at the
beach a few hundred yards from us. Only the intervening reef
kept the *Tagua* from scratching her keel against the pebbles and
dropping anchor.

"Let's swim in," Jakey suggested. "I'm tired of waiting. I
want to see what's on the other side of the island."

One usually has this feeling. The "other side" of the island,
on many atolls, is only a matter of yards. There usually is a
lagoon enclosed by more islands or another reef. But it is not
always the same, and the desire to find out about it was very
strong in us.

"Well, are you coming?" Jakey persisted.

"Don't be foolish! Papa wants us to look pretty when we meet
our new friends," Elaine said with a toss of her head.

"But look how clean and beautiful the ocean is. You can see
the bottom. There are no big waves breaking on the reef, and
most of all I think Papa will be pretty proud if we swim ashore.
The hell with you girls, I'm going now."

Jakey emptied strings, marbles, nails, and biscuit crumbs
from his pants pockets, opening and closing the blades of his
rusty pocketknife, thinking that this beautiful knife might
save his life from a hungry shark. He tied a string on the ring
at the end of the knife and placed the big loop around his neck.
Then he took off all his clothes, jumped onto the side of
the ship, and prepared to dive.

"Hey there, you goddamn Puka-Pukan savage!" we heard

Papa scream from the captain's position in the back of the ship. "You put on your clothes! You're no longer in paradise. You're in civilization!"

But Jakey's action gave Papa an idea, and immediately he started putting on a *pareu*. Then he jumped into the water and called for Jakey to join him. Jakey was over the side in a flash. Papa swam under water for about two minutes, visibly wiggling his tanned body in the glassy water.

"Esetera!" the cook yelled at the top of his voice to someone ashore. "There's a nice fish swimming toward you." And that is how Papa met our future mother.

Strange as it may seem to some people, our papa first asked our approval of his new wife.

"Look, kids, if you like her and you think that you will be happy with her, tell me now and I'll do my best to please everyone. After all, she will be one of the family; we shall live together in one house. Think hard, cowboys."

A few days later Esetera came to visit us, so that we could all get acquainted. I'll never forget the doubt in her perceptive eyes when she saw the four of us sitting stiffly under a bread-fruit tree, our mood openly critical. She was a young woman, about twenty, but quite mature in physique, as are most Polynesian women of that age. She had a sweet face and, as we learned later, a kind heart. Her philosophy was simple: Eat, sleep, and enjoy life. We liked that. The minute she spoke to us softly in Manihikian, a little like Mama, we looked at her with a kindlier expression. She spoke with such sincerity, her eyes sparkled. She was the true Manihikian woman, referred to in many books as the gentlest and most beautiful of all women in the world. The skin of her graceful, curvaceous body was light, and the coconut oil shone. When she kissed our cheeks she held us lightly, like a soft breeze brushing a gardenia petal. Even knowing that most Polynesian women are extremely jealous, we felt quite certain she was not that way.

But she must have thought Papa a weak father for having consulted us about his desire to marry her. Yet Esetera understood and was not at all like the mean stepmothers we had heard about from other people. Nga cuddled in her lap that same day.

When she had gone home, Papa watched us walk away to an isolated spot on the beach to make our decision. There, beneath a pandanus tree with hermit crabs crawling over and under it occasionally to wiggle their fragile claws as if they understood our problem and were giving advice, the meeting solemnly began.

We did not know the importance of marriage, nor did we know the rules involved. But we were aware of the fact that this woman was going to live with us, cook our food, help wash our dirty clothes, sleep with us, and sometimes go off alone with Papa on trips. We told each other our fears: maybe we would not be able to sleep with Papa any more, swim, take long walks, tell stories at night or our dreams to Papa in the morning during breakfast. It was sad to think we might never again hear Nga seriously tell Papa, "I remember when Jakey and I went fishing in his dream last night." "Yes, Nga," Jakey would agree, "we sure caught some pretty big ones." And we would try not to laugh at the little *potiki*.

We really did not need anybody to do the work, but we had thought Papa wanted a wife when he hinted that it would be good for us to have a mother. So we agreed in the end that it would be all right. It was fortunate that we loved Esetera.

The wedding was a simple one. It took place on the cement patio of the administration building in Tauhunu, the capital of or biggest village on Manihiki. Esetera's relatives, every single one of them, were there, more than happy because

Esetera was marrying a white man. The women dressed in simple white dresses, and the men wore white starched drill trousers since white is always worn on Sundays and holidays. They presented Papa and Esetera with mats and hats woven from coconut and pandanus leaves, and live pigs that snorted and poked their noses into the baskets of baked chicken and pork. The cooked food was delicious and abundant, and the leftover food was divided among those attending.

The long-awaited moment came when some of the natives began dancing to the quick beating of the drums and kerosene tins. Men and women bumped each other's hips as they wiggled their bodies and yelled for Papa to join the dance. Naturally, he got up and surpassed everyone with the wildest dance of the afternoon. With surprised admiration the natives watched the unusual way he wiggled his legs, sometimes knocking his bony knees together, his arms thrust way above his head, brushing the banana-leaf decorations hanging from the ceiling. And when Esetera joined him in the dance, he teasingly bumped her with his fast-moving hips. We kids joined in the dance when Papa called our names. But Jakey, who never liked to dance, hid in the crowd so that Papa would not see him.

Later the newlyweds and all the guests disappeared into the shade of the trees to rest, sweat running down their happy faces.

The first few months with our new mother were like a dream, the life one reads about in fairy tales. Esetera never raised her voice or lost her temper. She actually believed that a mother should play out-of-doors with her family as well as indoors. She went fishing with us. She taught us to plait hats, mats, and belts from young coconut leaves. She accompanied us diving for mother-of-pearl shells, camped overnight on remote islets, and sailed in our five-man canoe. She showed no sign of jealousy, even though we three girls were very jealous about Papa. Nor did she ask for special favors. She never once suggested that certain nights must be hers to sleep by Papa. She did not have to, for the two of them often quickly crawled out of the mosquito net and disappeared into the darkness. Only when we discovered the shredded and crushed leaves on the beach did we suspect where they had slept the night before.

We lived on the islet of Tapuaeka during most of 1942. It was one of the little strips of land that ring the lagoon of Manihiki. We had so much fun, it's hard to remember it all. I see all of us crossing a channel, with dried coconuts under each arm to keep afloat. Or again, I remember Jakey asleep on the beach, with a line tied to his big toe, awakening suddenly, pulling the line with all his might, and yelling till his face turned red. But he never wanted us to watch him haul in a fish unless he had seen in advance what kind it was. If it was merely a three-foot shark, he would twirl it around his head and throw it right back into the water with hidden embarrassment, before any of us saw it. (This was against Papa's wishes because he would have baked the shark's liver to get the oil from it for us to drink in the mornings. It was the best medicine for the teeth.) But if it was a big *ulua*, Jakey would yell, "Papa, Papa, Papa! Come here!" Immediately the typewriter would stop its clacking and Papa would run awkwardly to the beach, yelling, "Wow, wow, whoopee! There, Son, there! Esetera! Hey, you cowboys, hurry up and come here!"

But our visit on Tapuaeka was to end all too soon.

I often ask myself: How, if we had stayed there for only a short time, how could we have gone out night after night to catch wild roosters perched on the low *nonu* trees, or sailed our canoe time and time again to the outer islets, searching for birds' eggs, or made long hair out of shredded coconut leaves each day and each night placed it on top of the mosquito net? We made pancakes with animal shapes more than once; I know we did. So the only answer is: When one is very happy, time passes all too quickly.

Then suddenly our visit was over and we were sailing on Andy Thomson's boat, the *Tiare Taporo,* to Rarotonga, six hundred and fifty miles south of Manihiki.

CHAPTER 26

We Go to the Picture Show

The children are well. Johnny has become a little mathematical genius. . . . I am starting her in Algebra now, and I doubt if anyone else in this island can even solve A plus B. . . . Jakey is not much good in school, but he has a fine head for mechanics. I am, of course, giving him free rein. Better a good mechanic than a bad scholar. . . . Elaine also is no wonder in school; but she is fat and pretty and, I fancy, will make some happy man a very hot wife. . . . Nga (God bless her!) has chicken pox just now. She looks so terrible (just now) that I can see no future before her—barmaid, perhaps, or kitchen wench.

(Papa's letter to his brother, September 1943.)

Get up, kids! There's Rarotonga. Land ho! We'll be seeing Charles soon!" Papa called to us as we lay asleep under a pandanus mat that we used on deck to protect us from the night mist and spray.

Rarotonga was green and peaceful, awaiting the sun. The mountains seemed to float in the ocean, a garland of sea foam around their solid stems. The houses in the villages were still invisible over the long distance, but smoke from breakfast fires assured us there was life on the island.

It was truly a beautiful picture as we approached Rarotonga by sea. I wondered at the shape of it, so unlike the other Cook Islands; perhaps a little like Moorea, Tahiti's sister. The mountains are pointed and high, with sheer exposed cliffs like naked arms reaching for the sky. The puffy clouds sit on the tips of them as if playing some gigantic game, like "king of the mountain," until they are edged off or joined by others.

As we sailed closer to Avatiu, where the *Tiare Taporo* dropped her anchor in the opening between the reefs, houses and other buildings became visible. A. B. Donald, Ltd., was the first one we saw. We felt a sentimental attachment for this store which sent Papa to Puka-Puka in 1924. Soon we were nearing the jetty, where curious onlookers always gathered.

"There's Charles! Hey, Son! Charles! Charles! Here we are." Papa pointed to each of us and introduced us in a bellowing voice across the narrowing water.

As we transferred to a rowboat for the final one hundred yards, Andy Thomson was yelling instructions to the native sailors, the other passengers were calling to friends ashore, and the pigs joined in by grunting and squealing nervously. We had never seen Papa so excited as when the boat finally touched the jetty. He jumped ashore even before the lines had been secured and, running to Charles, grabbed him and lifted him up high in the air. Then he shook his hand, kissed him, and shook his hand again. Charles was nearly thirteen, and Papa was not quite sure whether his son was a boy or a man.

In spite of Papa's exuberance Charles only managed a shy, uncertain smile. He glanced constantly at Jakey, plans for the two of them probably already running through his mind. And doubtless Jakey was going to give us girls a difficult time when he got together with his new freckle-faced older brother.

Grandaunt Piki-Piki stood close by, crying from excitement and from fear of the possibility of losing her adopted son Charles. She was a nice little lady who immediately reminded us of Mama Tala. She was friendly to Esetera, but we could see that she was not very sure of a mother so young and so beautiful.

Esetera managed herself very well among the Rarotongan women in their formless cotton frocks, who stared at her in great curiosity. Many women said she was too young for a forty-seven-year-old man, and in loud, scarcely concealed whispers they predicted trouble ahead.

We rented a decrepit English house out of town, a big house near the water. For the first time in our lives formal schooling began for us. Every morning, we walked the three miles to the Catholic convent in the main town of Avarua, joining other native children along the way. The road was cut through thick trees and bushes, and we often ran half of the way, hopping and jumping on freshly fallen leaves and flowers to enjoy the sound of the crunching and crackling. Sometimes a rattling old truck slowly came our way, and if the driver was friendly we rode to school. Sometimes it was a noisy wagon loaded with fresh fruits and delicious vegetables, and we managed to fill our stomachs while riding.

Then Gene Autrey invaded Avarua one Saturday night. Papa bought the five of us tickets to the movie, instructing Charles to take care of us and keep us all together.

The theater was in an old warehouse. There were long, hard benches in neat lines, covered with dried chewing gum from past audiences. Even Cook Island youngsters cannot be controlled when it comes to gum and theater seats. We sat near the front and, looking back, could see a small balcony with a few chairs for the privileged whites or half-castes. At the entrance to the balcony sat a fat, short man, who Charles told us was Willie Brown. He owned the theater, but more important, Charles said, was the fact that he was also the man who explained the movie as it was shown, translating the dialogue into Rarotongan at the top of his voice. Charles then pointed out the projection room and the screen hanging on the wall. He did not forget to inform Jakey of the troublemakers who sat behind us so they could annoy us by pulling our hair. "They also like to poke their fingers in your sides when the movie is scary," he added. But since Charles was one of the best boxers on the island, we did not pay too much attention to the pranksters.

Soon the lights went off. The audience whistled and screamed and pounded their bare feet on the rough wooden floor. From then on there was rarely a quiet moment. The first thing we saw was a song movie, with the English words thrown on the screen. A ping-pong ball bouncing from word to word kept pace with the music. The house trembled with the un-trained voices of the audience. Charles sang, too, and we were surprised and proud of his knowledge of English.

Next a great big lion opened its mouth, growling and giving us suspicious looks. It was scary all right. I almost screamed with fright when Nga grabbed my arm and buried her head in my lap.

"Johnny, watch out!" she cried. "That thing is going to eat me!"

"Don't be silly, Nga. I don't think the animal can get away. He has a rope around his neck," I answered, but I was not certain myself.

The audience was whistling now, or growling like the lion.

Then horses came galloping straight at us, and Nga jumped up and climbed on my lap, yelling, "Move, Johnny, move! The animals will run over us!" This was enough to make everyone around us laugh. Even Charles exploded.

Often Willie Brown would loudly ask the people to quiet down so that he could explain more clearly what was going on in the mind of Gene Autrey.

Elaine and Nga fell madly in love with the hero, especially during the scene he searched for his loved one, singing, "South of the Border." For months afterward I, too, was very much in love with Mr. Autrey. Jakey reacted differently. He learned to make wooden pistols to tie to his belt, and constantly frightened us by jumping out of the bushes or swinging down from a branch, yelling at the top of his voice, "Stick 'em up!"

CHAPTER 27

Good-by, Esetera

. . . In the lands of the Anglo-Saxons there is a heritage of greed and jealousy which makes objectionable the thought of marrying a woman who has been loved by other men. This heritage has been developed through ages when the attainment of food, shelter, safety, a mate, has been consummated only by proving one's self superior to others. Civilized man has idolized private property; "mine" has become a sacred word to him; his pride has been injured and his safety jeopardized when others have conquered his property. His monoganic marriage is a direct reflection of his attitude toward property. . . .

(MR. MOONLIGHT'S ISLAND, page 158.)

Papa started writing *Amaru* again. We thought he would never finish this book, for we often saw him sitting despondently alone, pondering on what to do about Esetera.

On Rarotonga our new and precious mother had soon given us nothing but disappointment, and the village wags had plenty to gossip about. She changed from what she had been, a gentle, tender girl, into a philanderess, a drunkard, and a

good-for-nothing woman. Civilization had been too much
for her.

In the beginning Papa allowed Esetera to buy all the loud-
colored clothes and cheap leather shoes she wanted, although
we were not rich by any means. She soon started leaving home
every night and coming back the next morning with the poor
excuse, "I visited last night with my relatives." She scolded
little Nga for everything she did wrong, and complained the
few nights that she was home when Papa would not allow her
to sleep by him. She used to get up at night to awaken Elaine
or me when we were sleeping next to Papa because she wanted
to change places with us. She had become mean and nasty to
us, but we hoped that she would change back to her kind
Manihikian ways.

The climax to this problem came one afternoon after we had
been on Rarotonga three months. Papa had been in the
hospital, and one day came home unexpectedly, to find not a
bit of food prepared for our lunch. I shall never forget the disappointment on his face.

"How long has this been going on? Who cooked your food?
Where is that good-for-nothing bitch? Answer me!" I was so
frightened and startled I could not open my trembling mouth.
Then Papa said gently, "There is food on the stove; see to it
that the kids eat well."

While we were eating, Esetera came into the dining room
to eat, as she was in the habit of doing. But she never came
early enough so that she could help us cook.

She was wearing a tight-fitting, bright rayon dress. The
lipstick that was smudged on her lips was thick and amateur-
ishly applied. Her once-beautiful soft black hair was cut short.
I missed the braids that had formed a crown on her head. I
tried to remember her as she had been, but her eyes had lost
their sparkle. She honestly thought she was glamorous and

desirable to every man in sight. She smiled falsely at us and started to sit down, but sensed the antagonism in the room. "How's Papa?" she asked in a whisper.

"Papa returned home today and is very angry with you. You better not see him now. You better leave."

She screamed at me in Manihikian, "You're just jealous!" Then she surprised me by walking through the sitting room to Papa's side, smiling as she turned her back to us.

"What do you want?" we heard Papa bellow. "Why did you leave the children while I was in the hospital?" He spoke in broken English, so that Esetera could understand, and sometimes he added sentences in perfect Manihikian, for he spoke the language better than we, or any other white man in the South Seas.

"I didn't leave them," she lied without shame. "They didn't want me around."

I wish we could have told him what a fool he was to give her another chance. I wish we could have made Papa understand how we hated living in the same house with Esetera, cooking her food, straightening her bed, washing her dishes. Each night, she dressed and paraded in front of us, showing off the clothes Papa had bought her. And often she turned her powder-smeared face to us in a patronizing way as she asked, "This dress is beautiful, isn't it? Well, I'm going to visit my relatives."

After this incident at lunch there was a change in the family. We were not as playful and talkative as before. Even when we said good night our voices were stern, kisses meaningless. We cried every night for Mama, wishing she were with us. Day after day our morale fell, until finally we were quarreling, fighting, and blaming everybody for everything. Often Esetera attempted to get Papa drunk so that she could borrow money.

And when she came to the house, we left immediately, to wander off where even Papa could not find us.

But one day Esetera came to me, crying, "Your papa is sending me back to Manihiki!"

At first I could not believe my ears, but her tears looked real enough.

"I don't want to go back."

I felt sorry for her.

"I don't want to go back. My relatives will laugh at me. I'll be good, please!"

I can't understand you, I thought. You can be very nasty and yet be such a tender person. I can't really hate you, although I've tried.

"Your papa listens to you," she pleaded. "Tell him I'll be good from now on. He said it's all up to you." (She meant the four of us children could decide for him.) She cried loud and sincerely, her head on my lap, holding me around the waist, as Mama Tala had when we left Puka-Puka.

We gave her another chance, and I lied for the first time to Papa, saying we needed a mother. She stayed home all right, two nights in a row. Then she started gallivanting again, sneaking out of the house late at night. This was possible since Papa still refused to sleep with her. She used to come home before sunrise, thinking she had fooled us.

Two weeks later the schooner *Tiare Taporo* sailed for Manihiki and the lower islands, with Esetera as one of the unhappy, wailing passengers. We did not say good-by, nor even look at her. But Papa did, and we saw a great sadness on his face.

CHAPTER 28

The Slave-labor Gang

I fail to see why a man cannot bring up children as well as a woman, and now, after seven months' experience, I know that he can. All this "only a mother knows" is rubbish. A man is quite as capable as a woman, though usually he is too lazy to take on the job. Often he is better equipped. He is not apt to spoil his children by sloppy sentiment. He makes them self-reliant.

(Papa's letter to James Norman Hall.)

After Esetera left us, we moved to Aorangi Village, some six or seven miles from Avarua. There Papa resumed full responsibility for us: teaching us manners and helping us with our schoolwork.

I have not thrown away the duty calendar Papa wrote out for us. It made things easier for him as well as his children. This unusual calendar hung on the wall exactly where we could not avoid seeing it.

FRISBIE'S SLAVE-LABOR GANG

JOHNNY: Cook breakfast Wednesday and Saturday. Wash breakfast dishes every day. Keep kitchen and sitting room neat; cook lunch; wash her play clothes. Evening tea (dinner) on Wednesday and Saturday.

ELAINE: Cook breakfast Tuesday and Friday. Wash lunch dishes and dry; keep bedroom and Papa's room neat; sweeping, mopping, dusting; wash play clothes (hers and Jakey's). Evening tea on Tuesday and Friday.

NGA: Cook breakfast Monday and Thursday. Wash tea dishes and dry; keep hall and porch neat; mop, sweep, and dust. Wash Papa's and her play clothes. Evening tea on Monday and Thursday.

JAKEY: Cook breakfast Sunday morning. Keep yard clean. Attend bicycles; keep lamps clean and filled. Evening tea on Sunday.

PAPA: Eat ice cream, sleep, read, scold my babies and go to the movies with them.

Nga was still just a little girl, seven years old, but she was a wonderful cook and washerwoman. She cleaned the sections of the house as listed on the calendar, washed her own clothes, and cooked breakfast and dinner at the correct times of the day. We often laughed when she announced evening tea in a stiff and businesslike manner: "*Kai-kai* is ready! I'm going to the picture show right away. If you don't come now, I'm going to clear the table. So you better hurry!"

It was a clever way to force us to leave what we were doing, important or petty. For if we ignored her announcement, she would actually begin clearing the table. Sometimes she called for us while we were still in the shower, or swimming, and innocently expected us to be ready in a minute. Once she scolded Jakey, Elaine, and me for being late and promised, pointing a finger at us as Mama Tala used to do, that she would tell Papa the next time this happened!

"And poor Tuaine has been waiting outside for me to go to the show."

"Well, you didn't expect us to come running out of the shower with no clothes on and soap in our hair, did you?" asked Jakey. "You want us to eat with no clothes on? That would really be funny!"

"You could have hurried a little. You did not have to dance and sing all the time. Hey! You think Papa will get angry if I leave now?"

"Who's going to clear the table?" asked the practical Elaine.

"I'll do it when I come back tonight."

"If Papa finds out he'll get angry. And why do you tell Tuaine to wait for you outside?"

"She's afraid of Papa."

"Tell the fool Papa won't eat her!" Then noticing Nga's hurt look, Jakey added, "I'm sorry. I didn't mean to call her that, and I forgot she's your best friend." Turning to Elaine and me, he announced seriously, "Now, you two, we must thank the Lord for having sent Nga to us. Please hurry! She wants to go to the picture show."

Elaine was much more difficult to deal with when it was her day to cook breakfast and dinner. On Tuesdays and Fridays she also proclaimed herself the boss! We had to do precisely what she commanded. If we left the house to go any distance we had to tell her, *and* without sneers on our faces. We took orders all day long! During eating periods we were never impolite, for Elaine demanded the utmost in table manners. But we could not see why we should keep our elbows off the table and eat with our mouths closed.

"Don't talk with your mouth filled with food, Nga! Also don't giggle or make faces at the table!" Elaine reminded us all. "When I'm the boss, there's no poking out of tongues."

Sticking out our tongues at the table was a great pastime when Papa was not around.

At times when Papa ate in his room, Jakey sat at the head of the table and acted like the big boss. I can see him now, reaching across the table for a piece of bread, and Elaine shouting, "Stop! You ask me nicely or I'm going to tell Papa."

Elaine was not the mean and selfish type, she just wanted to be recognized as being in authority when it was her turn. She always ended up giving Jakey another slice of bread anyway, reminding him that he had better do the same when his turn came.

But there was no greater amusement than to be present when Jakey prepared dinner. His manner was very awkward as he set the table or lit the primus. Cooking was a very serious thing to Jakey. To see his lips pressed close together, as if it were a harder task to peel potatoes than to scrape the waste from an old battery, was enough to cause us girls to start giggling. Another source of laughter was the way he handled the silverware, setting the pieces in the wrong places, although he had been shown the correct way many times. And he seldom used salt or pepper in his cooking, although when he did we could be sure it would be much too much.

On Jakey's day to cook we were always early at the table, straightening the spoons and forks like fussy housewives, setting knives and cups in the right places, then resting our heads on the table and groaning as if dying from hunger, but giggling all the while. But sometimes he cooked dinner in the late afternoon and left the food to get cold while he swam for an hour.

If one of us happened to be his favorite at the time, he served her first, giving her a bigger portion of the food and having her sit by him. If an argument started, she was naturally expected to support him wholeheartedly. And arguments always arose during dinner hours when Papa was not around. During his absences we could do anything we pleased: slouch in our seats, crisscross our legs on the chairs, hold the forks upright, as if ready to stab the ceiling, and best of all and most fun, lean on the table with one elbow, cheek resting on the palm of the hand while eating with the other. It was Jakey's favorite way of eating. But we all knew better than to try it if Papa was around.

Not only did Papa encourage us in our cooking and eating habits, but he also insisted we learn to speak English. For most of our conversation was in Puka-Pukan, although we spoke Rarotongan to our friends and some Tahitian to visitors from French Oceania.

One day Jakey, Elaine, Nga, and I crowded into a little corner of the living room of our house to practice English. This was a result of Papa's announcement that he soon would conduct a little quiz in English.

We recalled those questions which he would most likely ask, then figured out and rehearsed the answers in English. We tried to recall every English word or phrase familiar to us, but sadly there were not many: "Okay," "sing me a song," "run away," "no damn good," and very few others.

Elaine, in her jolly manner, commenced the session and, standing bravely in front of us, asked in English, "You, little ding, how old is you?"

Nga looked at Elaine seriously and thoughtfully. "Ah, ah," she began, then turning to me for an answer, asked, "Johnny, me is seven *mataiti, e paa?*"

"Yes," I answered like an old schoolteacher, "*I am* seven years of age. And don't say 'me is,' *e?*" We laughed.

In a straight line and with earnest faces we marched to Papa's writing room, where bundles of papers were laid on the table or on boxes. Jakey, the announcer, started off. "Papa, you listen we speaky English?"

"Okay, cowboys, I will listen to you *speak* English, and make it good." His surprised face was eager, but a little doubtful.

Me: "Papa, I wanna go to the cinema."

"That's very natural coming from you, Johnny. I'll have to think about it."

Elaine: "Nga, how old is, is—ah—*are* you?"

Nga: "I am seven years of age." She emphasized the words "am" and "age" for the latter was a new word Papa had not heard from her before.

"Bravo!" He clapped his hands.

Jakey: "We speak good English, huh, Papa?"

"Fine! Wonderful! Delightful!" he commented, clapping his hands vigorously. "One thing, though, Johnny. You don't say 'I wanna.' And Jakey, Elaine, and Nga! Don't look so serious."

He pointed to the kitchen. "There's a little rock candy I've been saving. It's in the jar hidden behind the bully beef cans. Help yourself to *one* piece each."

CHAPTER 29

We Hike on Christmas Day

The tall green trees with wide curtainlike buttresses; lichen-encrusted trunks a hundred feet to the first boughs; monster orchids and ferns clinging to the damp bark; outlandish, reeking moisture; grotesque parasitic things hanging from the limbs like water moccasins; serpentine convolvulus twining everywhere. . . . There is no under-brush, no grass, only the crawling roots of the island chestnuts, the long lianas hanging from the branches, the strange silences and the strange noises.

(MY TAHITI, page 129.)

Since our first real Christmas on Rarotonga in 1943, I have not been able to forget the way Papa gave us our presents. The other high lights of that holiday—the pretty dresses worn by children to church and the exchange of simple presents of pandanus purses, mats, baskets of very ripe tomatoes, oranges, fine quality taros, and dried fish—were just a prelude to "Papa's Christmas."

On Christmas Eve, I had gone for an hour or so to the Manihikian settlement in Aorangi to hear the beautiful *himenes* (native versions of hymns). Everywhere there were preparations for the big feast the next day. Men were grating coconuts, squeezing the juice from them, and pouring it into bottles with a slice of precious onion to give it odor. This would ferment during the night and be used the next day to soak baked fish and taro. Some of the women were wrapping fish, chicken, and pork in banana leaves, putting them in the oven to bake overnight. Others were peeling the hairy skin of the taros and chopping them into squares. Then they poured coconut cream over the taro pieces and wrapped them in banana leaves for baking.

Everywhere young children were carrying baskets of pork and fish to take to their friends and relatives. In exchange they would probably be given pork and fish to take back, or maybe a can of corned beef from New Zealand, or some imported rice. There was always much exchanging of food on Christmas Eve and Christmas Day.

When I arrived at the Manihikian settlement, the food was already steaming in the *umus* and people were sitting around the fires of burning coconut shells. They were now prepared to practice their singing until the late hours of the night.

I cannot seem to find the right words to describe the *himene*. It makes the listener feel all the beauty of the islands, and all the sadness, too. It is a language through which the people express emotions so deep that normally they are unable or unwilling to speak of them to each other. But the *himene* lets these emotions out. It is much more to the islander than just a hymn.

I sat next to Esetera's aunt, leaning on her well-padded side, helping keep the mosquitoes away with a coconut frond. I thought of Esetera and of her beautiful soprano voice, and wondered how she was enjoying Christmas on Manihiki.

Early in the evening I was fetched by Jakey, and we walked

home along the beach, with the sound of singing still filling the night air.

"Do you think Papa brought us any presents?" Jakey inquired.

"I don't know. I sure haven't seen any signs of anything."

"I guess he didn't then, but that's okay. Maybe he'll remember next year and buy me that black pocketknife at Willie Watson's."

"I told Papa about the pocketknife."

"Then I *know* he must have gotten it for me! I bet he's hiding it someplace!" Jakey was extremely excited, and wanted to run straight to Papa and find out about his knife.

That night, after we were in bed, we sang with Papa a song he made up for Christams Eve:

> *"Santa Claus is a nice*
> *"Old Man*
> *"With a whi—te be—ard*
> *"And a re—d coat."*

"Now," Papa said, "I think that should make Santa Claus pretty happy. Shall we say our prayer?" And we recited: " 'The Lord is my shepherd; I shall not want. . . .' " Soon we were asleep.

"Rise and shine! Rise and shine! Merry Christmas, cowboys!" It was Papa's singing voice we heard through the door. He was singing in the cookhouse as he made smelly pancakes and home-ground coffee for breakfast.

We jumped out of bed to run to the door and stumbled in a heap over four bundles of presents wrapped in colorful *pareus*, placed at the foot of our beds. With frantic fingers we untied the knots of the *pareus*. I found yellow and red pencils, writing pads, a new green toothbrush, a brand-new slate and some slate pencils neatly tied with a string, a bottle of oil, a back comb with glass diamonds set close together on its back, and a jar of delicious hard candies that had more colors than a parrot fish. I looked at Elaine and Nga, who were laughing and examining their presents. They had almost the same things, but in different colors. However, Papa had made sure that we all got special things of our own. There were even embroidered handkerchiefs and cotton panties!

But Jakey! He was the noisiest of us all. He screamed with delight at his new three-inch-long black pocketknife. He also got a pair of goggles and the thick, paste-like hair oil that he liked so well, besides writing pads, slates and pencils, a tooth-brush, and a comb.

And Papa had composed stories for us to read, like Book One: *The Old Man and Mr. Walker*—a book for Johnny and Jakey and Elaine and Nga. Book Two: *The Zingaroo Tree and the Plausible Owl*. In Book One he included a song and changed it a little to fit Jakey's nickname, Hardpan Jake:

> *Oh, Hardpan Jake from the head of the Lake,*
> *With hair on his chest, that's me.*
> *I've pawed this earth from the day of my birth,*
> *With a spirit proud and free.*

It was the first time we had seen our names in print!

We washed our faces, combed our hair, put on our new *pareus*, then got Papa his presents, two green coconut mats, thirty-six by thirty inches, for his typing table. As we entered the aroma-filled kitchen we sang Papa's song about Santa Claus, who was a nice man and had such a white beard and a red coat. Papa was flipping pancakes without the use of a spatula. And with a fast turn of the pan the pancakes flew right onto our plates. As we ate we followed the usual routine, the telling of dreams of the night before. We were so excited, though, we made up most of our dreams.

We were a little suspicious of Papa's dreams, too, but we pretended not to be because they were so interesting and different we did not want him to stop. He would frequently tell about dreaming of the four of us kids doing fantastic things and saying new English words we had never heard before. And after we had heard about the dream, Papa made certain we learned the words.

But this Christmas morning Papa told us he had had the best dream of all the night before. "I dreamed that when we finished breakfast we took some food and left for a picnic in the forest and we did not even have to do the breakfast dishes!" Then he opened a basket. "Well, what do you know?" He looked at us with a sly smile. "Here is some bread and corned beef and water, just as in my dream. What are you cowboys waiting for? Let's go!"

The trail led off from the main road, about halfway from our house to Captain Andy Thomson's place. Soon we were walking through neat tomato plots, the bushes planted in perfect rows in the rich soil, a long stick tied to each plant. It was the season when the tomatoes had not quite ripened, and our mouths watered as we thought of the taste of a tomato picked and eaten fresh from the little bushes. We threw mountain rocks at the myna birds that sat on the trees waiting for the tomatoes to ripen. But we made certain we didn't hit any of the pretty things, for Papa had taught us that it was cruel to kill birds unless we needed them for food. Besides, they were so much fun to watch.

Climbing the foot of a hill, we crossed an unpaved inner road fit only for horse-drawn buggies and wagons. Guarding the road in orderly rows were mango, orange, coconut, guava, and *ii* trees. The *ii* has a clam-shaped nut which has to be baked in an underground oven and split before the delicious gray meat can be scooped out with a knife.

Soon, as we worked up the hill, we were puffing and speaking only in snatches. The lack of hiking during the past half year had turned us into weaklings. But we were very proud of Papa, for we had never seen any of the other white men take long walks in the valley or up the mountain. They usually rode their bicycles or drove cars to the canoe club on the windward shores when they went for an outing.

We sat on the rounded hilltop—half our bodies hidden in the dancing mountain ferns, our hair blowing about our faces. We could see the village of Aorangi below, our house with the red roof, and the store where we bought bread, rice, sugar, and tobacco for Papa. The ocean looked very peaceful as the sun burnished its surface. Minute toy figures crawled along the reef as they fished.

"Where shall we go next?" Papa inquired after we had thoroughly rested.

"Down that dark valley, Papa," answered Jakey. "There's a river and lots of ripe oranges." Jakey pointed to the valley on the inland side of the hill.

"Maybe we can find shrimps in the river!" added Elaine.

"Excellent! We'll make our own trail down. I'll show you how the American Indians make signs, so they won't get lost in the big jungles, by breaking twigs and laying rocks on top of each other."

We turned our backs to the ferns, and soon we were deep in the lush jungle bushes, which were damp and smelled of old soil.

We kids did not have the faintest idea of how to make an Indian trail in this green heaven, but as we walked on, Papa showed us how to break twigs in the direction of the trail we had left behind so they would point our way back. These he spaced fairly close together. When we found rocks we laid one on top of the other, with the top stone protruding back along the trail, pointing to the last sign. Papa said if we could follow these signs on our way back, we would be full-blooded Indians.

We worked downhill, sliding on old moist leaves, climbing over huge fallen branches, and crawling like true hunters through thick vine groves. The wind blew very strong through the tree limbs above, and the whistling noise from the long, skinny leaves of the ironwoods reminded Papa to tell us of Uncle Charles' cello playing. Occasionally we climbed into the trees and whooped with delight as we swung from tree to tree, landing on thickly entwined branches or, often as not, in a pile on the jungle floor.

When we reached the foot of the hill we sat by the stream to rest and scratch the mosquito bites on our arms and legs. It was a big stream, running swiftly toward the sea. We undressed and took a quick cold bath, searching for the shrimp that like to lie along the riverbanks. When we had collected a handful of shrimp we climbed ashore and dried ourselves by scraping the water from our bodies with the edges of crisp leaves. In Puka-Puka we used coconut leaves to scrape the water from our bodies, but on Rarotonga, where very few coconut trees grew, any leaf had to do.

Refreshed and cool, we started down a long unused path, playing a guessing game with Papa. He asked us to find a "stump" for him. Not knowing the word, we made wild guesses, pointing at boulders, coconuts, myna birds, and so on. Finally when Nga by chance pointed correctly at a stump Papa overwhelmed her with extravagant compliments, at the same time winking at us. Nga pretended she had known all along, and we pretended we were in on the joke, but of course it was just another way Papa had of teaching us a new English word.

During the height of the stump episode Jakey spotted a row of wild orange trees. Among their branches were beautiful clusters of ripe and green oranges. The colors were mouth-watering, and the thought that they were there for anyone who happened to be thirsty and that we could eat all we wanted made our thirsts seem unquenchable. While Jakey perched on a branch and peeled oranges with his priceless Christmas pocketknife, we sat under its laden branches and impatiently waited for him to throw down the sweet-smelling fruit. We kept Jakey very busy peeling oranges and throwing them down to us and each time he threw one down he yelled, "Merry Christmas, you all!" When we had had enough we faced the sea and began our journey home.

"Now, Papa, tell us about Uncle Charles in America!" Elaine reminded him.

"Yes," Jakey added. "Is he black, like us, or white as flour, like you?"

"Oh—first, he is a brilliant man. He likes to learn and use long words. He calls himself a lexiphanicist, one who uses long words. When he speaks, it is in a whispering voice, but his words are so clear that it would be impossible for anyone not to understand him."

"Does he dance and plays the guitar?" Nga excitedly asked, as she took Papa's hand from Elaine, the latter having had her turn.

"Please, Potiki. Does he dance and *play* the guitar?"

"Well, does he?"

"No, Nga."

"Oh." Nga sounded a little disappointed.

"But he is one of the best cello players in California. And he loves cats, especially Siamese ones. Oh! I see a papyrus plant. Which one is it, cowboys?"

This time we knew, because Papa made the mistake of looking straight at it. It was a rare plant on Rarotonga.

We followed the trail along the riverbank, and soon we were on the main road at the seashore, only two miles from home. We'd had a wonderful time, but we'd completely forgotten to return by way of the Indian signs.

CHAPTER 30

Voyage Interrupted

I rather enjoy roaming over the Pacific with my kids, and I fancy it is a better education for them than the ordinary schooling. They are becoming as multilingual as their mother was.

(Papa's letter to his brother, January 1942.)

By the end of 1944, in December, Papa decided to return to Puka-Puka. He was very tired of Rarotonga, and having finished *The Island of Desire*, he was free to sail again.

Papa had a big quarrel with Piki-Piki about her not allowing Charles to sail with us. She never let our older brother out of her sight for fear that we might kidnap him.

We set sail on the *Tiare Taporo*.

In order to pay half of our passage, Papa worked as the chief engineer. We discovered then that Elaine was a better sailor than Jakey, Nga, or I. She helped Papa check and oil the movable engine parts. She slept at night on the floor in that smelly engine room, next to Papa. There was always grease on their hands and clothes.

On the way, we stopped again at Manihiki. As we children were re-exploring the island we found Esetera sitting on the front porch of her home, which was connected to the parson's house. She was singing to a beautiful, well-oiled brown baby.

She had married a husky Manihikian Islander. She excitedly invited us to a Manihikian dinner, but we had to get back to the boat. When we left, she gave us a basket of food, consisting of baked chicken, drinking nuts, and dried *pauas* (mantrap clams). She was very jolly, as in the old days, and wanted to see Papa. But he was with Captain Andy Thomson and Dan Ellis, drinking bush beer. Before sailing he sent her some pretty things from our treasure box: combs, smelly soap, Three Flower hair oil, and Cashmere Bouquet powder.

We sighted Penrhyn four days later in the late afternoon of December 31, having come eight hundred and fifty miles from Rarotonga in about ten days. Captain Thomson decided to moor for the night outside the leeward reef. The passengers screamed with anger because they wanted to celebrate New Year's Eve on land.

All night long the winds carried the beat of dance music. The sharkskin drums shared their thunder with the sound of empty tin cans beaten by sticks. The music which resulted echoed off the cement wall of the old church and blended with the crash of the surf.

Sitting on the bowsprit, our feet pointing toward the dark sea below, we could clearly see people on the beach, most of them American soldiers and their sweethearts, some calling to passengers on our boat. They were so close to our schooner we could hear them speaking to each other onshore.

Very early in the morning, too soon after sunrise on a New Year's Day for most people to awaken, the *Tiare Taporo* sailed proudly through the reef channel into the polished lagoon and bumped her side against the wharf.

The first visitors to come aboard were the army officers, who seemed to have taken a liking to Captain Andy Thomson. They brought a case of whiskey and lots of American cigarettes. Then Philip Woonton, an old friend of Papa's and the captain's, joined the celebrants. They were drinking and singing songs when we went ashore. We wanted to see as much of Omoka as we could before the *Tiare* left for Puka-Puka the following morning. Returning to Papa late in the afternoon, we heard from the captain's room Papa's muddled voice: "Yes, Captain, I have decided to stay here with my family. These army officers need a sane American around. . . . Children! Cowboys! Get our things. We're staying!"

In the Tongarevan tongue Motu Toto means the "Island of Blood." It was on Motu Toto, a long, narrow strip of coral sand several miles long and covered with coconut trees, that we spent April through August of 1945. But first for three months we stayed in Mr. Philip Woonton's house in Omoka, the biggest and most modern village on Tongareva Island. The English called the island Penrhyn, in honor of its discovery in 1777 by Captain Stavers of H.M.S. *Lady Penrhyn*.

Mr. Woonton was a giant of a man. He was very dark, half Maori-New Zealand and half white, with a voice that surpassed even Andy Thomson's. He was a pearl trader by profession, but had the typically varied background of a South Sea adventurer. One of the few times I can remember him speaking in a moderate voice was when he suggested to me that the second of his seven children, his son James, would be a fine catch for a husband. "Yes, my boy Jamie is one of the best in the world. I have put aside thousands of pounds, and he will own this money when he is of age or as soon as he gets married. You will make a fine couple." Papa was outside, some distance away, making a stool for the kitchen, and later told me he could hear every single word Mr. Woonton "whispered" into my ear.

For many hours each day Mr. Woonton would sit on the patio of his beautiful home, staring at the never changing scenery of coconut palms and breadfruit trees. Since his patio faced inland, he could not see the ocean and the coral heads that rise above the lagoon at low tide. He would leave his long, hard bench only to walk down the stairs to the dining room, where he usually ate alone, or to walk a quarter of a mile to the w.c., built on a quay in the bay. Every four weeks he went down to the harbor to meet the *Tiare Taporo* when she made her regular visit. On rare occasions he might gather his older sons and their native friends to go sailing on his cruiser to the outer islets. He had worked hard in his youth, saved lots of money and, oddly enough, seemed to have found a true peace of mind.

We children liked Tongareva because of the American soldiers brought by the war. Twice each week we saw movies in their theater, and thrilled when the young soldiers offered to walk us home. We ate too many chocolate bars and hard candies, and this resulted in our first dental cavities. Along with the young Penrhyn Islanders, we tried to smoke American cigarettes and learned to apply lipstick and powder to our faces. Papa told us that if we did not stop such nonsense he would take us away from Omoka. When he saw that American-Tongarevan babies were arriving with increasing regularity and the island boys were stealing eggs to exchange for cigarettes and pocketknives, Papa finally decided to take us to Motu Toto, about three miles across the lagoon.

The islet belonged to Woonton, and in no time arrangements were made to move our belongings. We were very, very unhappy at first. We were angry with Papa, and spoke to him only when necessary. But soon we almost forgot Omoka across the lagoon and fell into our old pattern of living. We again started school under Papa's supervision.

In geography Motu Toto was altogether different from any other place we had lived. It had not only an ocean reef, but also a reef on the lagoon side, only twenty yards from the gravel beach, rich with delicious periwinkles and splendid cowrie shells. When the tide was low, the coral was at least two feet above the water and we could see the crabs in the crevices pulling in seaweed—or, sticking up in the air, the antennae of lobsters sending messages to their friends.

Our house rested on the water's edge. The bunks were built on the windward wall, where we had full advantage of the trade winds. Directly in front of the house was a quay built of huge slats of coral rocks, which we used as a platform to dive off into the clear lagoon water or to watch the big *uluas* and sharks swim by. At night we would lie on the flat rocks and watch the stars twinkle, aware of the fish lines tied to our big toes.

Further inland, close to the fresh-water well, was the cookhouse. From there we might walk only fifty yards before facing the other reef, on the windward side of the islet. This reef took a little longer to reach and was dangerous for the inexperienced. A half mile from the cookhouse a breadfruit grove mingled with the coconut trees. At night the wild roosters and their hens perched on the branches, heads tucked neatly under their wings.

Friday nights, when it was very dark, Papa led the way to the grove, making sure to follow the thick layers of coconut fronds laid neatly on the path so that we would not go astray. We marched to our usual posts around the trees. Jakey threw a big rock at the birds. With annoyed cackles, they flew blindly in the dark over and around us. Some of the birds bumped into trees and were dazed for a few moments. These were easy to catch. But the ones that kept running we would have to chase, barely seeing them, and tracking them mostly by the scratching noise they made. Those we missed would, without fail, hide in a fern grove or under a dried coconut frond. If we did not find them that night, we would awaken before sunrise to search these likely spots before the birds moved. Sometimes they would stay concealed all day, and when we found them hiding we would often feel so sorry for them that we would forget all about eating them and would try instead to feed and tame them.

Nga seldom caught anything, she was so young. But one night while we were in the process of hysterically chasing some birds, often as not slapping each other instead of the fowl, we heard Nga scream, "Papa! Papa! Papa!"

"Where? Where are you? What is it?" Papa answered as we all ran to protect her, Elaine, Jakey, and I thinking that she had seen a ghost.

"My legs, Papa! My legs! Something is there!"

She was so frightened and excited that she could not recognize the feel of this object.

Papa felt between her legs. There was a poor hen hanging by the neck, struggling feebly.

"Hell's afire, Nga. *You* caught a pretty big one!"

"Yeeeow! *I* caught a moa. *I* caught a big moa!"

We cheered and congratulated her, and I could see Potiki Nga's white teeth flashing in the dark.

Then there was the Sunday we picked periwinkles on the reef. People had warned us never to work or play on Sunday, but to read the Bible and sleep in the house or under the shady tropical trees. We should not even play cards or catch little fish to feed to our pet albatrosses and white terns. Papa did not believe in this blue law, and convinced us that there was nothing wrong with swimming across the lagoon or picking periwinkles to cook on hot stones. So this beautiful bright

Sunday found us searching the reef for interesting objects. About a half mile south of the quay Elaine gave a wild scream and dropped the hem of her dress, where she kept the periwinkles and sea shells she had collected. We ran to her and found that her forefinger was bleeding, the blood in the water enticing the very playful and cocky little white *maninis,* who seem to be giving orders with their mouths when one stares at them too long. They even made Elaine forget her injury for a moment, but when she thought of how much fun it would be to have Papa comfort her she screamed and asked us to take her home. Papa, of course, had run out of the house when he heard Elaine calling. He kissed her forefinger and sucked the blood from it.

"A little eel bit me. My finger is *mamae.*"

"Of course it hurts. Imagine a little eel like that biting my poor darling's finger. Now you go right on and cry. If you like you may cry very loud. I'll help you."

Together they cried, louder and louder, until Elaine burst into laughter. We all knew Elaine's finger did not hurt much, but we enjoyed the game she and Papa played.

But a month later Elaine barely missed the worst kind of accident, and this was not funny. We were gathering coconuts on the beach when we discovered human bones among the rocks. Some were half buried in gravel along the line of the shore. We collected some of the bones, mostly those of the arms and legs, and wrapped them in tunafortia leaves to bury under the coconut trees. But an awful thing happened. While Elaine was digging with a sharp, pointed stick, sweat mixing with the dust on her cheeks, an oblong coral stone was hurled at her from the bushes. It missed her head by a fraction of an inch. We became frantic, and immediately ran for home.

We did not tell Papa because we felt he would not believe our story, but we were sure an evil ghost had tried to kill or hurt

Elaine. After all, there was no one on the island but us. When later we told Mrs. Woonton our story, she revealed to us why people no longer lived on Motu Toto. Many years ago Motu Toto had been the big village and the capital of Tongareva. The inhabitants lived a happy life, fishing and making copra. They dug many fresh-water wells that were now dry, and planted many coconut trees. But one day an unknown sickness killed a large number of people, and they were quickly buried in shallow holes. This mysterious disease gripped the island for weeks, until those who were not caught in its deathly claws sailed by canoe or walked along the reef to Omoka, where they escaped and lived to tell of the plague of Motu Toto.

Mrs. Woonton also told us that, according to the native belief, if the rock had touched Elaine's cheek she would have died instantly!

Papa himself experienced a similar incident a few days later. We had walked, waded, and swam the six miles to Viggo Rasmussen's island, which was located on the same reef as Motu Toto. About halfway over, fever struck Papa. It slowed us a little as we had to carry him whenever we crossed the channels in the reef.

That night while Papa lay awake in Rasmussen's native hut he saw the light of bright lanterns circling a coconut tree outside. He watched in amazement, then awakened Elaine, who stared in fascination for a moment and then awakened us just as the mysterious lights suddenly disappeared. Papa had never seen anything like this before, and he tried to explain it to himself by telling us that it might have been a light from a ship reflecting on a rusted water drum outside. However, he decided to return to Motu Toto immediately after breakfast the next day.

We were happy to leave such a mysterious island, but we would miss the thousands of wide-awake birds we had dis-

covered there. The island was so thick with wide-awakes that
we could not have left if the white and gray birds had not
moved to give us walking space. The whole beach was covered
with their polka-dot eggs. We made a basket from leaves of
coconut fronds and gathered all the eggs we could carry to
take back to Motu Toto. For the next two weeks we fed on the
eggs baked in young coconut leaves and served them with
young *utos* and roasted albatrosses.

CHAPTER 31

Pago-Pago

Sweet Johnny,
Strong Jakey,
Happy Elaine,
Potiki Nga,
Dear Cowboys:
   This letter is from the big boss cowboy in the hospital in Pago-Pago. Kia orana kotou, i taku tamariki tikai [Greetings, how are you, my fine children].
   Meitaki au. Te noo nei au i roto i te are maki. Te kai nei au i te kai marie, mei te lollie e tai atura i te kapu ti [I am fine. I am in the hospital. I am eating sweet food, like lollypops and tea with lots of sugar].
   I will go back to Penrhyn Island and my nice children in maybe one month or maybe two months, and then we will all go on a ship and go to Tahiti and America.
   I have bought my cowboys plenty of pretty things, and some pretty things for Philip's children too. And I have bought charcoal iron [auri toka] for Dan and Tangaro and Torea and Hiro and Mommy Taira.
   Be a good girl, Johnny. Help Taira with the housework, and stay in the house at night. Then I will not worry about you.

Jakey, be a good boy and help Eliatara, and Philip.

Elaine, go to school and learn everything, and don't eat all Taira's food.

Nga Iti: Be happy, and win all the marbles, and don't quarrel with your brothers and sisters.

When all my big bad cowboys see their new dresses and their shoes and stockings and panties and perfumes and hair oil and Jakey's shirts, shoes for all of you and lollies and bottles of beer— you will be very happy.

Remember, while I am away, Taira is your mama and Philip is your papa. Do what they tell you to do.

Write me a long letter NOW and send it by the airplane. When I came to Samoa the airplane flew over Rakahanga. And it flew over Nassau! The islands looked like big green jewels in the blue ocean.

Viggo is with me in the hospital and he sends you his love and says you are number one cowboys.

I think about you sweet children all the day and I dream about them all the nights.

Goodnight, Johnny,
Goodnight, Jakey,
Goodnight, Elaine,
Goodnight, Nga,

Your foolish Papa.

After five months on Motu Toto we returned to "civilization" in Omoka. Once again we were unhappy to be moving, but this time for a different reason. Papa's health had been steadily getting worse. Soon after we returned, Papa began to have hemorrhages and the army doctor put him in the camp dispensary. I was allowed to live there and help watch over him. We had a pretty cottage. Our sheets were clean and changed every other day, and for a while Papa semed to improve. During this time I ate in the officers' mess, where I was escorted three times a day by pairs of serious-faced soldiers. At the mess I was very shy, and could barely speak even when spoken to. I was uncertain of my table manners, and so ate very little of the rare American food. The escorts, meanwhile, were always asking me to call upon them if I needed anything. Of course, they had nothing else to do, and one could see boredom on their faces.

"Now, little gal, if you need help, or if anybody gives you trouble, just you call on me."

The w.c. was built on high posts about thirty yards off shore in the lagoon, and whenever I walked on the quay toward it a couple of men would run to the foot of it to stand guard, so that no one else would visit the w.c. I was so embarrassed about this arrangement that in the daytime I sneaked into the bushes.

When Papa did not get well but continued to hemorrhage, the army doctor decided he must send him to the navy dispensary in American Samoa, or Pago-Pago, where he could have the many transfusions he desperately needed. Seeing the plane take Papa away gave us the worst feeling since Mama died. It was on that flight that Papa first met Mr. James Michener, author of *Tales of the South Pacific*, although they were to meet again later under more favorable circumstances.

While he was away in the hospital, we four children lived in one of Mr. Woonton's empty houses. We cooked and washed and usually went to bed at the right hour. When sometimes I sneaked out to one of the army dances, the officers would scold me in a fatherly manner: "You know that you are not supposed to be here. Now go home and look after your brother and sisters or I'll write your papa."

October brought good news: Papa was better and had sent for us! We had our first thrilling airplane ride. At the beginning it was very interesting, but when we got above the clouds we soon dropped off to sleep, Nga first, then Elaine and Jakey, and finally I.

When we landed at the airport in Pago-Pago, a familiar voice could be heard in the crowd: "There they are! My cowboys!" We were so happy to see him we all started crying. He looked well and happy, and his face was radiant as we ran to him. He told us that not only had he finished writing *Amaru* but it was to be published soon by Doubleday & Company. He was also teaching, and was the acting principal of the local high school for boys.

Papa was very proud of his school, and as soon as we were settled drove us out to it in a navy jeep. The school was located on a beautiful cliff, overlooking the ocean. The classes were taught in *falés*, or Samoan circular huts, built on little manmade hills. Papa told us that the *falés* were built round so that when the proud Samoan chiefs had their meetings they would all be in a circle and no one chief could be designated as the head man.

While Papa taught and wrote and Elaine and Nga tried to stay out of mischief, Jakey and I accepted an invitation to sail on the schooner *Samoa* to Olosenga, or Swains Island, about two hundred miles to the north of Pago-Pago and three hundred miles west of Puka-Puka. Papa let us go for a week, knowing how we loved to travel.

Swains Island must have been paradise for the swarms of mosquitoes there since they had an endless amount of tender pigskin to bite. We had never seen so many wild, reckless pigs on a tiny island, nor fought with so many mosquitoes. When we walked across the island to look at the outer beaches and be reminded of Puka-Puka we were several times chased up trees by wild boars. At night we slept buried in sand dunes on the beach, with only our faces visible. This way the mosquitoes could not bite our arms and legs. But, oh, our faces!

When we arrived back in Pago-Pago (Pago-Pago is pronounced like "mango" only with a "p"), Papa, Elaine, and Nga were ready to leave for British Samoa, seventy-five miles to the northwest. Papa was getting to know too many jolly U. S. Navy men who liked to have him go to bars with them. We were glad Papa was leaving a place that discouraged him from writing and spending time with us. Anyway, four months in Pago-Pago was more than enough for us, so we sailed on the old boat *Samoa* to Apia, British Samoa, on the first of January, 1946.

CHAPTER 32

Life on a Samoan Ranch

The whole difficulty with me at present lies in the enervating nature of the climate. One needs inclemencies to rouse one's system; too mild a climate is just like too lazy a life, it runs one's system down until he has to constantly stimulate it with drugs or alcohol to be able to digest anything whatsoever. I have no doubt but that a sojourn in America, or even in Tahiti, will do a good deal for me, with fresh foods, and a more bracing climate.

(Papa's letter to his mother, undated.)

Soon after our arrival in British Samoa from American Samoa, Papa made the acquaintance of Mr. R. Berking. It was not long before he and Papa had become fast friends in spite of having apparently little in common. In no time at all Berking invited us to come to live with him in his big house in Letogo.

He was a large, red-faced man who owned a big and beautiful ranch. During the war he was held a prisoner in a concentration camp in New Zealand, along with the many other Germans who had made the South Pacific their home. As in World War I, these men were automatically and immediately taken to prison camps.

I remember him as one of the great admirers of a woman's backside, the fatter the better. Even his horse loved his daily little pats and appreciative comments. "You have a nice round back there, my fine girl," he would tell her. When we knew him he was married to a stocky Samoan girl, but we heard he had once been married to a beautiful white lady whom he later divorced. He fed us fried cow brains, bloody roast beef, and raw ground-beef sandwiches with thick slices of onions.

And the raw food seemed necessary to feed his quick temper and fuel his great frame. He had the loudest voice I have ever heard, louder than that of Andy Thomson or Philip Woonton. His face turned tomato red when he bellowed. He would sometimes go to Papa when he got angry at his Samoan workers and shout, "These goddamn thieves! These homeless bums! Can you tell me why they are so lazy? They steal every tool, every string and rusty can in the house!"

But he was not a nasty man, even if he was impatient and swore like the devil. He and Papa had one of those sympathetic friendships that seem to grow so easily between white men in the South Pacific, isolated from their native lands. Actually they disagreed about almost everything, except the movies we saw on Saturday nights at the Tivoli Theater. They both raved in admiration over *Gung Ho* and *Good-bye, Mr. Chips* and both abhorred Westerns, which they nonetheless saw faithfully.

Our life with the Berkings offered new excitements. We rode horses bareback through the valleys to the waterfalls and fast-moving rivers of inland Samoa. There we left the horses to graze on the rich grass while we swam for long hours. One of our favorite pastimes was to sit just behind the base of a fifty-foot waterfall and listen to the roar of the water. Then, like salmon, we would dive through the thick sheet of water into the chilly pool.

We learned tricky ways of riding a horse, like sitting sideways, imitating pictures we had seen of Princesses Elizabeth and Margaret. Jakey became very lazy. Usually when Mr. Berking sent his son Ronnie and Jakey to the hills to round up a couple of horses we had to wait so long for their return that he would send me after them. With a paper bag of ripe lady-finger bananas I would hurry to the low hill where the horses grazed. There, half buried in the tall grasses, Jakey and Ronnie might be fast asleep. So I would lure the horses to me with the bananas, leaving the boys behind to finish their dreams.

"I'm telling you, Pa, we looked all over the place for the horses," Jakey and Ronnie would often say.

"Stop that goddamn lying and saddle those horses or you'll get a kick in the pants," roared the German in mock anger.

But behind all this fun our days in Samoa were clouded by growing problems. There was an uneasiness felt among us children: the unexpressed fear that Papa was working too hard. Even that he might die! He was spending many long hours on *Dawn Sails North*, at the same time helping me finish my book, *Miss Ulysses from Puka-Puka*, to be published later by The Macmillan Company.

Papa's right leg swelled often, and the high fever which accompanied the swelling made us frantic. Sometimes when he lay completely motionless on his wooden bed, exhausted from writing, his eyes closed and his mouth half open, I thought he might be dead. I would be reassured only by tiptoeing over to him to listen expectantly for his breathing. While he was working day and night on his last novel, *Dawn Sails North*, it was not unusual for him to collapse in a way which frightened us.

Writing this last book was the most tedious job Papa had

ever tackled, and certainly the most challenging. He was determined to make *Dawn Sails North* his best and greatest novel, to surpass *The Book of Puka-Puka* and *Amaru*. He was experimenting in this book with new sentence structures and new words. When he slept he dreamed of new ideas to add to his novel, and would awake in the middle of the night to write them down on paper. He wrote these notes by dim candlelight while we slept nearby. Awakening in the mornings, I skimmed over the handwritten notations and the instructions on his clipboard. There were also corrections made on the pages I had typed the day before. By noon I had typed the usual fifty or sixty pages for Papa to work on that night. But it was not all that simple. Papa made many changes. The novel was typed over six times, and when he finally finished it I actually knew by heart some of the chapters.

Anyone who came to see us when Papa was at work was given very short shrift. Unless it was Berking, Papa would tell the visitor in a gruff manner that he was too busy to talk to or see anyone. And what moods possessed him! When he was greatly involved in a love scene, his face mellowed and he asked for the eraser in a whisper. But when he was working on a dramatic scene he would shout when he was disturbed.

Once he asked me, "How do you create a mean and nasty old man? Is it true that it is like giving birth? Do I have to go through the pain to create one? I'll never be a writer." But when his character had come alive, he marveled at it and whispered, "No, Johnny, Lee Barker can't bawl me out for this type of creation."

But Papa was wrong. When the "great novel" was completed in 1948, a story of romance, philosophy, and adventure in the South Seas, with just a touch of mystery thrown in, Mr. Barker asked Papa to cut it.

In a letter to Papa he wrote: "It is necessary to take out about ten thousand words in order to get it down to 125,000 words. That seems to be our limit these days for a three-dollar novel."

Papa was deeply discouraged. He threw up his arms and bellowed, "He is asking me to ruin this book! I can't do it!" But he did what his editor suggested. He eliminated much of the novel's philosophy and put in its place a stronger story. Papa was certain that *Dawn Sails North* would never be the great South Sea novel he had dreamed it would be. However, when Barker received the revised manuscript he wrote: "I'm sorry that I had to put you to so much work on *Dawn*, but I think you made a swell book of it and in the long run you will be glad you made the revisions. It reads ever so much better now."

And Barker kept after Papa, offering faith as well as criticism. In a letter written in 1948 he said: "Again I would like to suggest that you start your thinking about the next novel now and start working out a detailed outline. . . . There is no question but that you can write like an angel, that you know the South Sea Islands and their people as few men ever have, that you have an eye for the color and atmosphere of the islands, but you will still never become the great author I know you can be unless you work on combining these ingredients into a first-rate novel." Still later he wrote: "Don't feel you are fighting it out alone. You have some good friends and a lot of ardent fans in this country."

Yet Papa did feel alone more and more. Not only was he still broke and in debt, but he worried that we children would stop loving him.

"Johnny, do you hate me?" he once asked. "Don't hate me, please. I am this way because I want to make money to buy you and your brothers and sisters pretty dresses and shoes and take you to America. We'll go to Hollywood and meet the movie people. And I'll take you to the big libraries and opera houses. And if our money is plentiful, we shall sail down to the Caribbean, for you kids will love it there. Someday I shall make this miserable life up to you and your little brother and sisters."

He did not seem to realize that it meant very little to us to have dresses and fancy shoes. Yes, we wanted to see America, but longed even more to have the fun we thought we had lost with him. We had never seen him work so hard.

"Johnny, Jakey, Elaine, Nga!" Papa one day in January 1947 called. "Sit on the floor and listen to me. We have just enough money to fly by plane to Tahiti and visit Hall, whom I have not seen in over ten years. I've got to see him about a new book. Are you ready to travel again?"

"When?" we screamed at the top of our voices, running toward him with outstretched arms.

Within a week we had packed our trunks with books, manuscripts, and some few pieces of clothing, and had sent them by boat to Tahiti. Flying over Letogo, we spotted the pastures and the little hills of the Berking ranch, and we could see the tiny horses grazing in the huge front yard of his home.

We stopped a week on Borabora, which was as far as the plane went, and were taken on a grand tour by Papa, who knew the place well. We borrowed an old army jeep left behind by the American soldiers and drove as far as the unpaved road would allow. Papa showed us each place he and Mama had lived, camped, or picnicked. We met some of Papa's old friends, who, when they learned of Mama's death, wept shamelessly, muttering how gentle and kind she had been. They looked searchingly at Elaine, Nga, and me in the hope that they might see traces of Mama.

After a week had passed quickly, we spent a miserable night sailing to Raiatea on a small power boat. There were not enought bunks for everybody, and we had to try to sleep on the deck of the cabin. But it rained, and we went below, where we all got sick from the stuffiness.

At Raiatea we lived in an old European house surrounded by big trees and protected from the strong mountain wind by a fern-covered hill. We were happy to find this home away from the town, which was very dirty and unattractive. Two miles down the hill, beside an isolated pier, lived Charles Brown, his wife, and son Bob. The reader may remember that Charles Brown was one of the three men who founded the "South Seas News and Pictorial Syndicate" with Papa. Twenty years later we found him middle-aged, retired, and surrounded by his books. He kept in touch with the outside world through a "ham" radio set, which had become his pride and hobby.

The first Sunday we visited them the Browns served a delicious Polynesian banquet: raw fish marinated in lime and mixed with coconut cream; *poe*, a gelatin-like combination of mashed bananas and cornstarch, baked in banana leaves, which one dipped, before eating, in coconut cream; and *pota*, baked chicken and taro leaves in coconut cream. We drank fresh coconut juice while Brown and Papa sampled home brew and rum punch.

But Papa was getting impatient about seeing Hall and Spies. So after two weeks we bid the Browns an abrupt farewell and sailed on the rolling two-masted schooner *Moana*, sleeping on deck among bundles of bananas, seasick women, and snoring men.

Arriving in Papeete, worn but heady with excitement, we quickly set about to surprise Papa's old friends with our sudden appearance. But Papa was sad to learn that James Hall had gone to California to be at his daughter Nancy's wedding. Whitney Jones, another old friend, had died of a heart attack the day before our arrival. However, Spies was still at Papeari, in Tahitian country, living a retired life. And Andy Thomson was in port on our old friend the *Tiare Taporo*. He had come south to Tahiti, as many of the ship captains did during the hurricane season.

Again Papa fell ill, worn out by the trip and all-night reunions, and soon found himself in the same hospital where I had been born fifteen years before. He was very bored and unhappy during his two weeks in bed, and swore whenever the doctors visited him and did not give him medicine to ease the pain in his stomach. So when he heard that Andy Thomson was taking the *Tiare Taporo* to Rarotonga he set about convincing the doctors that there was nothing much wrong with his system after all. They willingly discharged him from the hospital.

"There is Papeete." Papa spoke softly to us on the deck of the *Tiara Taporo* as we watched the lights fade away to the east. "The only value that place has for me now is the memories of days past, which I'll never see again." Then without waiting for the island to disappear he went below.

CHAPTER 33

A Big Man-of-War

*. . . All activity stops while a ship is at an island. Barrels of
coconut beer are made, innumerable pigs and chickens killed.
There is feasting, yelling, drinking, riot. Drums beat in the
jungle at night. Flaring torches flash on the reef. It's all something I can't comprehend. Perhaps when I have left here it will
be like some weird tale I have read.*

(Papa's letter to his brother.)

The people of Rarotonga must have prayed extra hard at
church the day before. For the beginning of this Monday
morning in June of 1948 was extraordinarily beautiful. I had
just celebrated my sixteenth birthday a few days earlier. On this
particular Monday the people of Rarotonga were intoxicated
with excitement.

A New Zealand man-of-war had come to Rarotonga! There
was going to be a football game in Avarua, the capital, a cricket
match in Avatiu, and a tennis game at the Queen's Palace.
All my friends, and my brother and sisters, had made plans
weeks in advance to try to see all the games. But when Papa

had asked me just a few days before to accompany him to the afternoon tea at the Resident Commissioner's home, to be given in honor of a visiting New Zealand governor and his wife and officers, all thoughts of cricket or football were forgotten.

We had been asked to attend the biggest party of all! This surprised Papa, for an invitation to such a function rarely came his way. Everyone who was invited had known about this tea long in advance, and for months the women had been buying and sewing for the big event. One woman had even asked the Resident Commissioner if he would radio the man-of-war to stop at Samoa to pick up a package consisting of two brassières, so that she could wear a new one to the party.

Papa had made no such elaborate preparations. He wore an old pair of sandals, as he intended to be comfortable in his tropical clothes, even though everyone else would be stiffly proper. He helped me choose a light blue material for my dress. It was a beautiful dress, mostly because he suggested that we line the neck and skirt with white lace. He boasted that I would have the simplest and most beautiful dress at the party.

Thus attired on the great day, we climbed aboard our bicycles, which Jakey had vigorously polished that morning, and set out for a sample of Rarotongan high society. Guests on their way to the gathering passed us in rattling old cars, others were in fancy new Chevrolets from America, and a few rode in horse-drawn wagons. The wind brushed our faces and mussed our hair. I think everybody thought we were eccentric, going to the tea party on bicycles, and we occasionally heard giggles from the Rarotongans or received patronizing looks from some of the *popaas*.

As we pedaled down the dusty road we passed native girls dressed in their best; hair oiled and carefully combed, so that it would stay pretty; eyes sparkling, clear and bright as the sky. Young men sat on the roadside or roamed the streets to keep watchful eyes on their girl friends, young sisters, and mothers.

Arriving at the Resident Commissioner's house, we brushed the dust from our clothes while Papa remarked again how pretty my new dress was and strolled over to the front yard, where many people we had not seen in months were already grouped around the punch bowls.

We listened politely as the Commissioner introduced the officers from the man-of-war. To broaden my education in such matters, Papa pointed out certain members of the gathering.

"Look, Johnny, see Mrs. X flirt with that officer? Look at him wink back. Hey, there's a phony character sitting on a bench by that tree! She really must think she is somebody of great importance."

I felt a little ashamed because I thought that some of the people had heard us make fun of them. When it was time to leave, everybody gathered in a long line to shake hands with the visiting Governor and his wife. Papa and I were last in line so that we could watch the people.

As we moved closer to the head of the line, I became fascinated by the way the Governor's wife constantly jogged her head sideways each time she shook hands, and the way the great straw hat that shaded her perspiring but smiling face flopped back and forth.

We were the last to leave, filling our pockets with cookies for the rest of the kids. Mr. Bond the photographer asked how I liked the party.

"Well," I answered, "it wasn't very much fun."

"Johnny!" Papa whispered while the questioner looked somewhat amused. "That isn't exactly what you should say. Say something like, 'I had a wonderful and enjoyable time. The cookies were delicious, too.'"

I felt a little silly, but did as I was told.

As we rode to a friend's house where Papa and some cronies

were planning a little party, he laughed and laughed. "My own daughter saying that! What nerve. I'm proud of you!"

That night, Papa and his friends drank so much I had to pedal him home on my bicycle. The bicycle wobbled and bumped. Sometimes I had to get off and push it, one hand holding Papa up, the other holding onto the handle bar. Jakey and Nga came to my rescue when we arrived at home, puffing. We undressed him, leaving on only his skivvies, as he called his underwear. (Such a funny name, we thought.) He fell sound asleep and started snoring a little. Jakey wet a towel to wipe the perspiration from his face before we kissed him good night. Very much later we retired, hoping he would feel fine the next morning so we could all go swimming, enjoy breakfast together, and tell of our dreams.

But an hour later Papa called for us in a weary voice. I heard him crawling out of bed, and went to touch his arm. He asked for the rest of the kids, and I said they were asleep.

"Why aren't they here?"

"But, Papa, they are."

"Jakey! Elaine! Nga!"

"Yes, Papa," three whispering voices came out of nowhere.

"Come here!" he demanded, seeking the end of the bed for support. Three figures in striped and baggy pajamas hesitantly walked forward. Elaine, the bravest of all, came close to Papa and embraced his legs with her arms.

"Ah! This is my little Niu Papaku, (Elaine's nickname, meaning, Dried Coconut). You always take care of me, don't you, Elaine?"

"Yes, Papa," Elaine whispered very sleepily.

Then I stupidly added, "Papa, shall we put you back to bed?"

Face stern, like that of a man giving a campaign speech, arms locked in an attempt to pull his body into a sitting position, he distinctly asked me, "Don't you like to *talk* to me? Is that all you want me to do, *sleep?*"

My brother and sisters gave me scornful looks. Papa started muttering to himself, and we could not understand what he was talking about. Soon Jakey, Elaine, and Nga disappeared.

I was a little afraid, but came closer and rested my hand on his shoulder, pressing him gently to the kapok mattress, covering him with the sheet, and hoping he would soon sleep. But Papa was not ready to sleep. Steadying himself on the night table, he clutched the white sheet around himself and got up, stumbling around the dimly lit room like a specter.

Another of one of those nights, I thought. Might just as well prepare myself for a long and rambling conversation.

An hour later he was still sitting on the floor, leaning against the bed, and delivering a lecture on writing, sickness, poetry, and parental responsibility. He spoke of his longing for Puka-Puka, the *Motuovini,* and Mama. Finally the words trailed away into meaningless mumbling and his head fell forward.

I whispered to Jakey, who was hiding behind the door, Nga, cuddling close to him, head on his shoulder, and to Elaine, squatting behind the piano. They came to me, hesitatingly, to help carry him back to bed. He was heavy, but we were not entirely unused to this chore. After tucking the sheet around him we sat on the other bed and waited. It was so quiet the only sounds were our breathing and the noise of Touser and Trigger, our black mongrel female pups, hissing and blubbering as they dreamed under the bed.

Finally Jakey whispered, "Let's go and get some sleep. I think Papa's all right now." He took my right hand, and we all tiptoed outside the house like escaped convicts in the night. He led us to a big jasmine bush that was in full bloom and provided shelter from the night dew. Elaine and Nga were soon fast asleep in each other's arms.

"Jakey," I whispered, "Papa sure looked funny running around in that sheet, didn't he?"

I listened for an answer. It came, but drowsily. "I feel sorry for Papa; you shouldn't make fun of him." And I felt ashamed.

The next morning, the sun shone so bright its rays penetrated the jasmine bush and awakened us all. Jakey, leading the way toward the lagoon, was followed by the rest of us as we crawled out of our nest.

We swam, dressed, cooked Papa's breakfast, wrote a note telling where we would be, and left the house to meet our friends.

The day was uproarious, with drums and tin cans being beaten. We joined a large group going aboard the New Zealand man-of-war for a visit. Soon Elaine and Nga were giggling and pointing to all the sailors as they walked by. Jakey stayed as close to me as a crab to its shell, protecting me from the harm he suspected must lurk on this mysterious ship. He was afraid someone might grab us and pull us through one of the secret doors that led below, where no visitors were permitted. I laughed aloud at his fears, but did not feel too secure myself, and felt much better when we were finally off the ship.

At four o'clock we met Elaine and Nga and exchanged stories of our adventures on the big man-of-war. But soon we became serious. We wondered how Papa was, and began to worry about having left him alone for so long. What if he were really sick and needed us? Potiki Nga started to cry.

"Oh, be quiet! Nothing's wrong with him," growled Elaine, the optimist in the family.

Touser greeted us first, her long black tail wagging so fast one would think she had not seen us in months. We practically ignored her as we hurried through the patio and into the bedroom, to discover an empty bed. Then we heard the tinkling of pots in the kitchen!

There he was, our wonderful papa, dressed in brown khaki pants and a red-and-white-checked shirt, his short black hair neatly combed back. We watched with relief and joy as he set the table, placing the spoons and knives carefully, each time smiling as if he had accomplished something important. Then he turned, grinning. "Well! There you are! Tell me what you did all day. No, look pretty first."

It was a delicious supper, and a long one, too. Papa remembered what had happened the night before. From the manner in which he spoke and played with us I could tell that he was apologizing. "Please, my beautiful babies, forgive me. I'll never drink again, never!"

Papa kept that promise. He kept it till three nights before he went away, never to return.

CHAPTER 34

Charles and Jakey Go
to New Zealand

*I wonder if I shall see the old USA again. With a family of
daughters each year increasing my expenses by the only law
of the square, about all I can hope for now is to marry them
off in eight or ten years and then retire to one of the unspoiled
atolls—if there are any left by that time.*

(Papa's letter to his brother.)

I tell you, kids, the longer I stay in these so-called more civilized islands the more I long for Puka-Puka or Manihiki. And
if I don't make more money than at present, we can't go on
living here, in half poverty."

Papa was not the happy man he used to be. As we grew
older we seemed to have become more of a problem, one that
he was becoming less able to handle by himself. And being
in a more civilized land, we did less together. Brother Charles
had a job in Willie Watson's store, so we saw little of him.
Papa was corresponding with Mr. Alf Rowan of Epsom,

Auckland, New Zealand, a horse trainer who wanted Charles to come to New Zealand to work for him. For as well as being a champion boxer Charles had gained a reputation during the Christmas races as the top jockey in Rarotonga. It seemed likely that Charles would be leaving soon, and the four of us decided to spend a few days with our older brother.

Early the next morning the jagged and pointed mountains behind us were half hidden in the anchored clouds—I could not see the familiar line of our narrow trail circling the fern-covered ridges. Already there were early risers from the village of Atiu starting their daily climb to the banana and orange plantations on the hillsides, to gather the fruit and cover the sunburned roots with rich soil.

Charles lived with Auntie Piki-Piki at the head of a valley at the base of three connecting hills. There at their feet two waterfalls met in a pool. Piki-Piki's house sat on the bank, a simple thatched-roof house with movable shutters on the wall. Taro patches formed a muddy fence all around it, and the running stream at the doorway provided water for drinking and bathing. The stream itself was full of tunas (fresh-water eels) and large shrimps. Nearby there were mangoes and coconuts and numerous candlenut and guava trees. Behind them in the forest were wild roosters and untamed pigs.

Papa would have loved seeing this paradise, we thought, for it resembled so nearly the valley in Moorea where he and Mama had once lived many years before.

On this visit we met Charles' foster father, one of the biggest Polynesians I had ever seen. His life had been spent as a whaler throughout the world, and his stories surpassed even those of old William on Puka-Puka. But he talked very rarely, for he was half paralyzed and suffered from palsy. We children had never seen him before.

Old Piki-Piki fussed over us as Mama Tala often had,

fixing special taro foods and killing a few of her choice hens. But she was not a very happy woman, for soon her adopted son would sail away on the *Maui Pomare*.

In the early mornings, at the time the wild roosters hunt for their food, Charles led us a short way into the forest to show us how he trapped not only birds but small pigs to augment Auntie Piki-Piki's table.

"First," he said, "we take a strong bush, like this one."

Charles held the bush steady in his left hand, and with a butcher knife borrowed from the kitchen began trimming off the foliage until just the main stem remained. While he chopped, Charles lectured.

"For the trap we need a good strong stake that will bend. Now we could have brought one with us, but this bush is better because it has roots and won't pull out if a baby pig gets caught in the trap. *Kua Kite Kotou* [You understand]?"

We nodded, fascinated by his knowledge of woodcraft.

"Now watch!" he commanded. To the end of the bush he then tied a string, fashioned a noose trap with the loose end, and then pulled the stem over to the ground with the string.

The bent stem became taut as a bow. Charles then secured the string loop by pounding bent twigs around it into the ground. If a rooster or piglet disturbed the trap, the twigs would be loosened and pulled from the ground by the pressure of the bent-over stem. The noose would instantly close tight around the intruder as the bush sprang upright.

"Now let's scatter some food on it and cover the trap with leaves."

We did as we were told, happy to be able to help. Then Charles said we must leave it unguarded since a rooster will not come to a trap if people are around.

All that morning, we wanted to go back to the trap to see if we had caught anything, but Charles would not let us. Finally, in the late afternoon, we persuaded him to go. When we were close by we heard a squawking and beating of wings.

"We got one!" cried Jakey, and we all ran on. But when we got to the trap, Little Nga said dejectedly. "It's only a *manu kavamani* [government bird]."

And so it was: a half-grown myna bird, indignant and impatient at the loop tightened around his leg. After much beating of wings and abusive bird talk as we freed him, the myna happily flew away, never to be fooled by a bird trap again. We did not tell Charles, but I know Jakey was thinking, as I was, that we could have done a lot better throwing stones.

In the afternoon, when the sun had warmed the streams, we felt with our fingers for the shy shrimp that lived among the tree roots, hiding in the debris and crowding into the little caves on the stream bank. At night we sat on the riverbank, fish line in hands, each assigned by Charles to different tuna hide-outs, to await the pull of a fresh-water eel. This was the most beautiful part of visiting Charles' home.

From the darkness we could hear Piki-Piki's crackling, high voice while she talked to herself as she helped her husband to bed. Then she would be yelling for us to return to the house and say our prayers before going to bed.

We returned to Avarua and Papa. A week later Charles left. For days Jakey fished alone on the reef, and when he brought us his catch he swore that if Charles had been with him his luck would have doubled.

Papa still worked on *Dawn Sails North,* although at a very slow pace for the pains in his stomach occurred often. However, by my sixteenth birthday, in June of 1948, Papa had sent off the last of *Dawn Sails North,* and he and I then started writing a novel based on the lives of some people we had known. This was very slow work, for Papa was busy preparing Jakey to join his brother in New Zealand. Jakey, too, was to be trained as a jockey.

Dear Jakey looked forward to seeing Charles, but I often heard him crying at night at the thought of leaving home and Papa. He told me that he did not think he could live without Papa, and that Papa would be lost without a young man in the house to fill the kerosene lanterns, clean the yard, and help straighten out his three daughters. He asked me to promise that I would take good care of Papa; that I would mind him and help him with his writing.

In October 1948, Jakey went away and it was my turn to cry.

Papa became very quiet and withdrawn after this, almost as if he had lost another Mama. It was harder than ever for him to write. Instead we went to the movies many times, and visited friends in their homes. He promised us that he would never again part with one of his children.

CHAPTER 35

We Lose Papa

*The old man looks long across the lagoon and reminisces on
his past futile days. Then he wades in until the water comes
to his shoulders. He swims with long strokes until he is a mile
or more from shore and quite exhausted, and realizes that now
it is absolutely impossible for him to return to shore. He rolls
over on his back and stares heavenward, then he looks to land,
and suddenly he smells the fragrant mountain wind, sees the
beauty of the moonlight throwing the shadows of articulated
ridges across the water . . . he for the first time in his life
realizes that there is beauty. The desire to live, to enjoy this
beauty overwhelms him. He knows he has not strength to
swim to shore. He shouts, struggles. Then the dorsal fin of
the Monarch of the Pass cuts the water in a circle about him.*

(Papa's letter to his brother, Tahiti, 1927.)

November 17, 1948, was a day of cool, dead calm. All afternoon Papa and red-faced Andy Thomson had been drinking
home brew made in an unclean kerosene can. Their songs and
roars of laughter announced to the neighborhood that "Ropati

has broken his promise to the kids." But Elaine and I were unhappy, not angry. We had not really expected Papa to stop drinking forever. We knew how sick he had been lately and how lost he felt without Jakey.

Papa and Andy told each other the same stories they always told when they were together, their hilarity rising higher with each one. Soon eyes were peeping over the windowpane and children were crawling under the house to listen.

"Hey there, Johnny, get us another bottle, and make it snappy."

I went behind the closet to get a bottle of beer, counted what was there, then looked under the beds to count the other bottles. There were sixteen, but when I returned to the living room I announced, "Papa, you only have three left." He didn't even realize I was fibbing because I wanted the drinking to stop. He nodded his head happily and threw an arm around my shoulder, smiling proudly at Andy.

"Hey, wouldn't it be dandy if one of my daughters married one of your boys? Wouldn't we be proud men, admiring them as they walk down the church aisle? Hey, sea devil, I don't think Johnny likes this conversation!"

I walked outside, embarrassed, but I could still hear them talking. Their mood had changed, and it had grown quiet inside the house.

"You know, Andy, maybe Johnny *should* get married. She's old enough. I married Nga when she was fifteen. Besides, there should be somebody to take care of the kids if—I weren't around any more."

"Hey, you son of a gun, what kind of talk is that? Nothing's going to happen to an old salt like you. Have another beer!" They tried to regain their joviality, but soon Andy was saying good-by.

"Come over next week and I'll have Mama Ngarangi

[Andy's wife] cook us a dandy dinner." And Andy climbed on his old bicycle and started off unsteadily for home, ten miles to the leeward side of Rarotonga.

Elaine and I helped Papa into bed, washed his unshaven face, his feet and arms with a wet towel. Last of all, we kissed him good night and crept quietly out of the room to our beds. We said our prayers and asked God to make Papa happy.

Several hours later I was awakened by moaning. I rushed to Papa's room, where I found him writhing on the bed, his face covered with sweat and his eyes full of fear. They seemed to say, "This is it, Johnny, this is it!" He could not speak.

"Papa!" I cried. "I know what you're thinking, but you are not going to die. I shall see to it that you will live as long as you want."

Soon he fell asleep or became unconscious. I did not know which, and this frightened me. I thought of how Mama had died in his arms. I could no longer hold back the tears. Suddenly Papa sat up and groaned deeply.

"Johnny—don't ever—leave me!" he managed to say. It was a weak voice, a voice forced through the set teeth of lockjaw.

"Papa, what's the matter?" I asked, trying not to cry.

"Get—the—doctor." The words came haltingly. As I stood up, he held my arm and with his other hand pointed to his mouth. I did not comprehend at first, but when he pointed to a handkerchief I understood. At first I could not open his mouth, but finally with all my strength I pressed my thumbs on both his cheeks and managed to pry the jaw apart a half inch or so. Then I stuffed the handkerchief between his teeth so his mouth would stay open. Awakening Elaine and giving her instructions to watch Papa, I left to fetch the doctor.

My thoughts were in a turmoil. I thought of Jakey's first letter to me, which had arrived just a few days before:

"Dear Sister Johnny: I arrived in Auckland yesterday.

Brother Charlie and Mr. Rowan met me at the airport. . . . Be good to Papa, please, for I can't get him out of my mind. . . ."

If only Jakey were here now! I thought.

At the doctor's house I could hear nothing except crickets. I knocked at the door of the bedroom, but no one answered. I started to yell. The doctor's wife called out, "What the hell do you want?" but her voice was not unkind.

"My papa is sick."

"Again?" she answered, recognizing my voice.

"Papa wants to see the doctor."

"Okay, go back and tell him that I'll be there!" the doctor himself answered.

I pedaled home again. The moon had gone behind a single dark cloud. I passed a cemetery, and did not dare look back for fear of seeing the white headstones standing in ghostly rows by the hundreds. Papa was still awake when I arrived, Elaine supporting him by the waist. I took her place and was shocked to feel his hot, sweaty forehead and hear his heavy breathing.

"The doctor will be here soon, Papa," I told him.

He put his head on my shoulder, held my hand tightly, and unclearly whispered, "Johnny, Elaine, come here. I don't want to die! I don't want to die now! Please, God, let me live a little longer!"

"Papa, you won't die! You won't die, Papa!"

Weak as he was, he managed to squeeze my hand and pull Elaine closer to him. Nga was still asleep.

"My little babies, I love you. Take good care of your sisters, Johnny."

Then panic crossed his face and he tried to get out of bed. He struggled to sit up, and I felt his back muscles writhe spasmodically. Gradually he gave up, and I felt his body seem to grow heavier as slowly he realized that he could not make it. Elaine began to sniffle. She moved closer to him and asked, "Papa, can I do anything for you?" He shook his head and put his hand on her bare shoulder.

We waited for the doctor. We waited and waited. Finally at four in the morning he came and gave Papa shots which made him relax a little and gave him strength.

"Doctor, how long will this last?" Papa asked.

"You'll be all right by tomorrow," the doctor assured him. He left soon after and promised to send an ambulance first thing in the morning.

Elaine and Nga went to school as usual the next morning.

I sat by Papa's bed, and we talked about the book we had been working on together. But he grew steadily weaker. At ten o'clock in the morning I went to the hospital to get the ambulance. I told one of the drivers that Papa was really sick. They promised to send an ambulance, and I went home and waited by Papa's side until two o'clock in the afternoon. Then, in despair, I went to the hospital to again beg them to come.

Late that afternoon, I was ready to take Papa to the hospital on my bicycle, when, at last, the ambulance arrived. The half-caste driver and I carried Papa's stiff body into the ambulance on a tarpaulin stretcher and drove in silence to the hospital. Papa could not speak. The nurses and doctors took over then while I sat outside, hair uncombed, face unwashed, miserable and sick. I would not leave the hospital, and a New Zealand nurse finally had to chase me out. I walked home, not recognizing the people I knew, not hearing when they asked the usual, *"Tiane, pe ea koe?"* All I could think of was Papa.

Our house had changed. The rooms seemed colorless and empty. I ran to his bed, laid my head on his pillow, and smelled the sweat of the night before. I was nervous and afraid. I went into his workroom and stood by the wall, hands pulling my hair like a wild dog tearing at a coconut. Then my eye fell on the family picture he kept on his desk, the only one taken of all of us. Nga was sitting on Papa's lap, Elaine was on one side of them, and Jakey and I were on the other side. How happy we had been.

Later, when Elaine and Nga came home, I tried to tell them the whole story calmly and without crying. We ate dinner, washed dishes, and went to bed early, feeling each other's comfort.

It was a very quiet night—no stories, laughter, or pillow fights. We wore Papa's pajamas so we could feel him near, pressed our heads against his pillow, and even kissed the bed sheets where he had lain. Elaine and Nga cuddled close to me.

Thinking of Jakey's letter, I fell asleep and dreamed a strange dream. Papa, Jakey, and I were standing on the foredeck of a steamer, sailing slowly through a narrow river passage, barely wide enough for the ship. Suddenly we came to a dead stop. It was the end of the river, and we got off to investigate.

"You two go on," Papa commanded. "I'll stay on board."

We looked at him curiously, wondering, because this was the first time he had wanted to stay behind. Ashore, we looked back to see the ship sailing away, with Papa standing alone, waving at us.

I awakened. My first thought was to get on my bike and pedal to the hospital as fast as I could, but something kept me in bed. In spite of Papa's years of trying to teach me otherwise, I still could not forget the native superstitions. To dream of a ship is to dream of a coffin. When someone stays on that ship, that person is doomed to die.

Next morning I sent Elaine and Nga to school. Then I went to see Andy Thomson and tell him about Papa's sickness. I was talking to Andy on the *Tiare Taporo* when we saw an ambulance in front of our house, not more than two hundred yards away from the little jetty that stood out into the harbor. I heard it honk its horn and saw it drive slowly toward the jetty. Somebody yelled to me, something about being wanted at the hospital. I kissed Papa Andy good-by and paddled the dingy ashore.

I went to the driver, and as he opened the door for me a young native boy giggled, "Your papa is dead." I just looked at him, studying his face to see whether or not he was joking. "You're lying," I answered.

"Ask the driver. Isn't it right that her father is dead?"

"Don't scare the poor girl," the driver said as he backed the car around.

We drove to the hospital in silence. When we got there, people looked at me curiously. I wondered why, and thought it unusual. I walked into the hall, and a nurse led me to Papa's room. I saw a screen in front of his bed. As I always did, I rushed to his bedside, and saw only the white sheet drawn up over him. When I looked under it I could see that Papa was lying quite still, not even breathing. It took me several moments to realize what this meant. Then I collapsed on the bed, my arms around his waist, my face on his still covered face. I was aware of the other patients around, but I couldn't stop crying.

I hugged and kissed his hand, rubbing it with my tears in the belief that they would stay there forever with him. The nurse tried to take me away, but I would not go.

"Don't you see that he is dead? Can't you understand that I'll never see him again? Can't you leave me alone with him? Please leave me alone!"

She said that it was time for me to go, and I wondered why there was a time to depart. I stood up and told the nurse that I wanted to see Papa just once more. She nodded her head. I lifted the sheet and looked at his face. It was that of a sleeping man. It reminded me of a time in Puka-Puka when I saw him sleeping and thought he was dead. Now he *was* dead, and would no longer speak to me except in my thoughts. I kissed him for the last time.

I saw Papa's face just once again, when he was buried; I had made a *yei* (wreath) and put it in his coffin.

Sometimes I see Papa eating happily across the table as he once did, occasionally looking to see if we are watching our manners. And sometimes I seem to hear him say things he should not, when I am talking to pompous or self-important people.

I wonder what he was thinking just before his last breath of life. Mama must have been there to help him. I only wish that Nga, Elaine, Jakey, Charles, and I had been with him, too, for as I once said to him long ago, "Papa, we love you as long as it is permitted."

Epilogue

The reef welcomes yet resists the crushing power that moves over it with an exploding roar as the wave sends spray crashing high into the air, forming a brief rainbow in the sun, while the swell, its power spent, rolls quietly now into the haven of the deep lagoon.

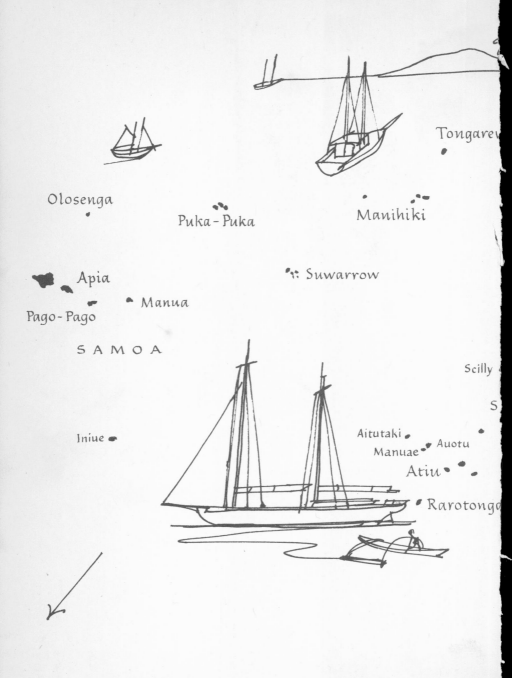

Tongare

Olosenga

Puka-Puka

Manihiki

Apia

Pago-Pago

Manua

SAMOA

Suwarrow

Scilly

S

Iniue

Aitutaki

Manuae

Auotu

Atiu

Rarotonga